Interdependence

Interdependence
Renewing Congregational Polity

A Report by the Commission on Appraisal,
Unitarian Universalist Association

June 1997

Unitarian Universalist Association
Boston

Copyright © 1997 by the Unitarian Universalist Association. All rights reserved.

Unitarian Universalist Association, 25 Beacon Street, Boston, MA 02108-2800.

Cover design by Charlotte Burgess.
Text design by Suzanne Morgan.

Printed in Canada.

ISBN 1-55896-358-8

10 9 8 7 6 5 4 3 2
00 99

CONTENTS

Preface and Acknowledgments	vii
Introduction	1
Part 1: Congregational Polity in Theory and Practice	5
1. Theological Perspective	7
2. Unitarian Universalist Tradition: A Short History	17
3. Comparative Congregationalisms	31
4. The UUA Bylaws: A Study in Ambivalence	41
5. The Spiritual and Cultural Ethos of Unitarian Universalism	51
Part 2: Pressure Points: Issues and Concerns Related to Congregational Polity	63
6. Congregational Governance	65
7. Cooperative Relationships	79
8. Communications	95
9. Religious Leadership	105
10. Social Justice	123
11. Marginalized Groups	133
12. Internationalism	155
Conclusion and General Recommendations	169
Toward a New Community of Autonomous Congregations	

PREFACE AND ACKNOWLEDGMENTS

Interdependence: Renewing Congregational Polity has been prepared by the Commission on Appraisal of the Unitarian Universalist Association. The subject of this report is basic to both the spiritual and the institutional life of the Unitarian Universalist movement, as described in the Introduction. Detailed recommendations for various groups within the Association are given at the end of each section, and these are drawn together in the Conclusion as a set of basic recommendations for study and action.

This is the ninth report published by the Commission since its inauguration under the Bylaws of the UUA in 1961. The Commission consists of nine members; three are elected by the General Assembly every other year for six-year terms. The Commission is charged with reviewing any function or activity of the Association that it believes would benefit from independent review and with reporting to the General Assembly at least once every four years.

After the publication of its 1992 report, *Our Professional Ministry*, the Commission began to solicit the concerns of a broad range of people and groups within the Association. This process involved meetings requested by various groups, meetings with denominational leaders (usually at the Commission's request), unsolicited requests and suggestions for topics of study, and open hearings at General Assemblies and in the various locales of the Commission's meetings.

During the period of this study (1992 through 1996) open hearings were held annually at General Assemblies of the UUA. Open hearings were also held in the Pacific Northwest, Prairie Star, Mid-South, Southwest, Ballou Channing, Mass Bay, and Pacific Central Districts. Meetings with the Commission were held with the following groups: Women and Religion Committee; Gay, Lesbian, and Bisexual Ministers; Young Religious Unitarian Universalists; Unitarian Universalist Young Adult Network; Unitarian Universalist Urban Ministry; University of Minnesota Unitarian Universalists; African American Unitarian Universalist Ministry; and Ministers of Religious Education.

Consultations were held with the following UUA officials: former president William Schulz, President John Buehrens, former moderator Natalie Gulbrandsen, Moderator Denise Davidoff, Executive Vice President Kathleen Montgomery, Vice President for Development Robert Snow, Director of Ministry Diane Miller, Special Assistant for Interfaith and International Activities Kenneth MacLean, Director of Publications Patricia Frevert, Ministerial Settlement Director Daniel Hotchkiss, Director of Annual Program Fund Mary Miles, and district executives and consultants as a group. Consultations were also held with Rebecca Parker, president of Starr King School for the Ministry; Spencer Lavan, former dean and CEO of Meadville/Lombard Theological School; Professor James Luther Adams; and Professor Conrad Wright. Correspondence was also received from many other individuals.

Writing a report such as this is a complex task that requires the help of many people. The Commission wishes to express its deep appreciation to Wendy Drexler, our editor, and the staff of the UUA Department of Publications: Patricia Frevert, director; Brenda Wong, project editor; Suzanne Morgan, design director; Joni McDonald, production manager; and Scott Brigante, former production manager. We also appreciate the assistance of John Buehrens and Denise Davidoff in enabling the timely publication of this report in spite of budget constraints.

This report has multiple authors. Each of the Commissioners wrote specific sections, and all commented on and improved on each other's work. We take joint responsibility for the endeavor. The current Commissioners appreciate the work of the former Commissioners who contributed to the early stages of the report but whose terms expired before publication: Florence Gelo, Philadelphia, Pennsylvania; Charles Howe, Raleigh, North Carolina; and Amy Kelly, San Francisco, California. We also thank John Buehrens for his active interest in our work; as president of the UUA, he is an *ex officio* member of the Commission.

The Commission invites comments on this report, and on other matters of concern to the Association. Written comments or inquiries may be addressed to the Commission on Appraisal, c/o Unitarian Universalist Association, 25 Beacon Street, Boston, Massachusetts 02108.

Dianne E. Arakawa
North Marshfield, Massachusetts

David N. Barus
New York, New York

George Kimmich Beach
Falls Church, Virginia

Marjorie Bowens-Wheatley
New York, New York

Lisa Presley
Southfield, Michigan

Gustave Rath
Evanston, Illinois

Deborah Roberts
Shreveport, Louisiana

Arthur J. Ungar
Lafayette, California

W. Frederick Wooden
Brooklyn, New York

Introduction

One of the deepest convictions that unites us as Unitarian Universalists is a belief in the possibility of a beloved community among people, whether members of a family or the most diverse representatives of humanity. We affirm that such communities are in part a natural outgrowth of human life, but that they must also be deliberately formed and reformed, nurtured and renewed.

This is a spiritual vision that eludes precise definition. It is no wonder, then, that we speak of this vision with differing accents. We speak of unity in diversity, of the community of love and justice, of the kingdom (realm) of God. Our UUA Principles speak of the interdependent web of existence of which we are a part. James Luther Adams spoke of the covenant of being. These terms express a vision of the individual person and the community of persons in harmony with each other, the world around us, and the spirit of life itself.

Unitarian Universalism seeks to embody this spiritual vision and to advance its fuller realization. We seek a way of being in the present that leads toward the future. A primary way that we try to embody our spiritual vision is through the congregation, the face-to-face community of people who seek to walk together faithfully, courageously, and joyfully. We want our religious community and the network of relationships that extends beyond itself to be a living model for the good of human relationships throughout life.

However, our institutional ideals and practices have lagged far behind our spiritual vision. In particular, "congregational polity" has been used as a shibboleth against the fuller recognition of our interrelationships. It is the central thesis of this report that the idea of congregational polity needs to be revised and, indeed, re-visioned among us.

Community and autonomy do not exclude one another, but enhance one another, for the essential function of the congregation is to link the individual to a religious community.

We are calling, then, for a new way of thinking about who we Unitarian Universalists are and what we seek to become. As we do so, we will reshape our shared vision and our practices to reflect this vision. We will alter the ways in which we relate to one another, make institutional decisions, and seek to implement policies; we will alter the content of our teachings and the spirit of our celebrations.

The Commission believes that we should honor the congregational heritage of the Cambridge Platform of 1648, recognizing that it upheld a vision not simply of congregational autonomy but, as Conrad Wright emphasizes, of "the community of autonomous congregations."

There is inherent tension between the concepts of *community* and *autonomy*, similar to the often-expressed tension between responsibility and freedom. However, community and autonomy do not exclude one another but enhance one another, for the essential function of the congregation is to link the individual to a religious community. It is to mediate between the individual and the "church universal." It is to link the local congregation with other congregations and indeed with peoples of faith universally.

This report examines congregational polity as the principle of organization to which the Unitarian Universalist movement has been committed, and the ways in which our understanding of this principle influences our practices. The report highlights the major tensions between congregational polity, as it is commonly understood among us, and current institutional practices and developments that do not fit well with our polity.

We take our commitment to congregational polity as an established principle. We recognize that this principle is deeply rooted in our sense of the local congregation as the center and spring of our vitality as a religious movement. But we also note that, because of our strong emphasis on individual freedom and local autonomy, the associational dimension of our congregationalism has tended to be ignored. Seldom do we preach about congregational polity or even teach it, except to accent local autonomy. But every time we call a new minister, or vote on a resolution of ethical witness, or give money to denominational bodies, or receive financial or expert assistance from a denominational body, or deliberate our ministry to the larger community, or question standards and practices that are commonly honored, we touch on issues of congregational polity.

We often feel a tension between the association of congregations and the autonomy of the local congregation. Sometimes that tension is unavoidable, but often it results from a failure to consider fully the integrity and vitality of both.

Beginning a Conversation

The Commission believes that we need to modify our understanding of both the theory and the practice of congregational polity. The spiritual vision of our faith and its institutional agencies require it. In short, in our thinking about institutional life and relationships, we are calling for a paradigm shift from individualism to interdependence, from the autonomy of the congregations to the community of autonomous congregations.

In our understanding, the term "congregational polity" signifies a network of independent congregations, working for both their individual best interests and the best interests of the Association as a whole. An important part of such a network is stronger lateral relationships among congregations, helping to overcome the temptations of both isolationism and centralism.

We are not proposing something new, but are seeking to revive awareness of what was central to congregational polity from its origins among our denomination's New England forebears. For the Cambridge Platform did not view the local congregation as going it alone, but accented the community of autonomous churches. The Platform spoke of six ways in which congregational churches exercise their responsibility to and for one another: care, consultation, admonition, participation, recommendation, and relief.

Today these six ways remain valid as guides for creating a community of autonomous congregations. In fact, "care," "consultation," and "participation" are often richly acted on today, except among those who need it most—alienated or isolated congregations. "Recommendation," "relief," and "admonition" are infrequently acted on, perhaps because of an exaggerated belief that such actions would infringe on the rightful independence of another congregation. The UUA itself approaches these matters with great caution, for the same reason. And yet there are many instances in which the internal difficulties of a congregation—for instance, financial need, conflict over a minister, or exclusionary practices—could be immensely aided if local congregations saw themselves as mutually responsible to and for one another. The Commission believes that the future integrity and vitality of the Unitarian Universalist movement depends most directly on deepening our sense of mutual accountability.

Forms of organization and governance go to the heart of our identity as Unitarian Universalists. They express and influence the tasks we take seriously, support, and celebrate. Our polity is the institutional means through which we express our Principles and Purposes. Clarifying and renewing our understanding of congregational polity are therefore vital if we are to realize the vision espoused by the Principles and Purposes.

The future integrity and vitality of the Unitarian Universalist movement depends most directly on deepening our sense of mutual accountability.

The Commission on Appraisal hereby asks the UUA, its congregations and other constituent groups, and its individual members to begin an in-depth conversation about our unwritten constitution: congregational polity. This discussion must include the most important but often overlooked element of polity: the responsibility of congregations to be in right relation within themselves, to one another, and to other communities beyond the Association.

PART ONE

Congregational Polity in Theory and Practice

The five sections of Part One speak to five basic dimensions of congregational polity: theological, historical, comparative, constitutional, and cultural.

1. Placing congregational polity in theological perspective clarifies the basic meaning and value of congregationalism as an expression of our spiritual vision.
2. Understanding the history through which this form of governance has come down to us illuminates present institutional commitments and forms.
3. Describing congregational governance as practiced by other religious bodies provides useful comparisons with our practices.
4. Analyzing relevant provisions of the UUA Bylaws reveals both common understandings and tensions in the relationships between the Association and its constituent congregations.
5. Examining how our colloquial understandings of congregational polity enter into the spiritual and cultural ethos of contemporary Unitarian Universalism profoundly affects our sense of identity and shared purpose.

SECTION ONE

Theological Perspective

Being part of a religious community is a personal commitment that reflects a theological vision—namely, a sense of the fundamentally interdependent, or covenantal, nature of existence. Being in community, then, is not incidental to being a Unitarian Universalist, but intrinsic and inescapable. The religious community is the vital matrix of the formation of its members' diverse personal ministries. In turn its members reshape the community. This section examines the theological implications of congregational polity in terms of a new understanding of our central mission: the shared ministry of the religious community in service to the world.

Talking with newcomers about the Unitarian Universalist faith, we often emphasize that ours is not a single, centralized *church*, but an *association* of churches and fellowships. In other words, our denominational structure, the UUA, is a voluntary association of independent, self-governing congregations.

Usually we call these religious communities churches, but sometimes we call them fellowships, societies, or congregations. Sometimes we simply call ourselves "Unitarian Universalists," suggesting that no adequate term for the group exists, or perhaps that here we are individuals, first and foremost. And sometimes we use the term "parish" to refer to a local congregation, although parish properly refers to the geographical area covered by a congregation. The lack of common terminology, in part rooted in our dissenting tradition, tends to confuse discussions of the basic meaning of being a religious community. A congregation may serve many purely social needs, but first and foremost it must serve our need for a spiritual community, a community of mutual commitment, caring, and support.

The idea of absolute or total independence, congregation by congregation, is impossible insofar as the principle of congregational polity must itself be agreed on by a collectivity of congregations.

We need not adopt any one term for our religious communities, but we do need to understand that commitment to a local, face-to-face religious community—a congregation—is intrinsic to our faith. We may share an understanding of sociological, historical, and organizational perspectives on the religious community. But because we are often radical individualists for whom religion is a private or an inward feeling, a *theological* perspective on the church (the religious community) seems incomprehensible to us.

Toward a New Self-understanding

We need a new or renewed doctrine of the church—a conception of religious community that is integral, not incidental, to our total theological understanding.

The Commission believes, however, that a renewed theological understanding of the religious community—an awareness of why "being in community" or "covenanting" or a lively sense that "the interdependent web of all existence of which we are a part" is central to our faith—is key to reaching a fresh and liberating understanding of congregational polity itself.

Our denominational name—Unitarian Universalist Association—itself reflects the centrality of congregationalism to our self-understanding. When we accent the word "Association," we invoke the concept of congregational polity. We are proud of the tradition of local independence that congregational polity represents, and we often suggest that this form of governance is more in keeping with our beliefs and values than any other form; it is more democratic, free, and respectful of local autonomy. We have tended to think and say that the right of a congregation to do whatever it chooses is the hallmark of true (or pure) congregationalism and that to stray from that principle is to violate something sacred that makes us what we are.

On the other hand, we are restive with this self-understanding; stated in this strict form of self-autonomy, congregational polity does not adequately reflect our sense of who we truly are. In some of our practices, we have largely abandoned this ideal in favor of identification with "Unitarian Universalism" or some other trans-congregational term. A notable example is the practice of ordination to the ministry, where the ordaining congregation is the ordinand's "home" church or "internship" church, rather than a church that is also calling the ordinand to be its minister. The practice reflects our sense of being part of a religious community rooted in, but not limited to, a particular time and place, to which we are called in ministry.

Few of us would hold that "the church"—in the sense of the religious community to which we are devoted—exists *only* on a local level, in the congregation. In fact, in the Universalist tradition, ordination was not enacted by local congregations, but by state conventions. And in the Unitarian tradition, although ordination was originally enacted only by the local congregation that was calling the ordinand to its ministry, all Unitarian congregations recognized the validity of each others' ordinations.

The idea of absolute or total independence, congregation by congregation, is impossible insofar as the principle of congregational polity must itself be agreed on by a collectivity of congregations. In some sense this collectivity is "the religious community" and *is*, or at any rate *represents*, the church as a spiritual body, something that transcends the local, gathered church community. The Puritans who wrote and subscribed to the Cambridge Platform of 1648 did not themselves hold such a purely congregational notion of the church, however wary they were of hierarchical or clerical control; they held that the church was, "in matter," the elect of God, and "in form," the covenant of believers in Christ.

Toward a New Doctrine of the Church

If, then, "the church" is more than the local congregation, what is this more? How do we name it? Theology has become attenuated among contemporary Unitarian Universalists, especially in terms of a common faith. Thus it is extremely difficult for us to reach a theological consensus or even to agree upon a common language of faith. We need a new or renewed doctrine of the church—a conception of religious community that is integral, not incidental, to our total theological understanding.

A completely "de-theologized" notion of congregational polity—one that speaks of the church in purely sociological or historical terms—makes nonsense of the idea itself. Thus if the idea cannot be theologically renewed among us, we will finally jettison it as an encumbrance or absurdity. The *reductio ad absurdum* of this way of thought is to say: The church is a club for our kind of people, and it matters little whether you think of it as a debating club, a social club, or a political club.

Unless we can put congregational polity in theological perspective, we will not be able to resolve the questions of practice that arise around it. (Part 2: "Pressure Points: Issues and Concerns Related to Congregational Polity," addresses these major questions of practice.) A serious discussion of congregational polity leads us—perhaps surprisingly, but inevitably—into renewed theological discussion touching many broader issues of faith.

Six Propositions for Theological Reflection

The following six propositions trace the major lines of theological reflection on the nature of religious community.

Congregational polity is not, and could not be, the sole possession of any one congregation.

1. Expanding our concept of governance.

Polity refers to forms of governance, and governance is one of the central questions of religious reflection, that is, of theology. Hence we ask: How is the universe governed? How will I govern myself? How do we agree to govern ourselves?

These three questions exemplify the complex set of questions that can be asked about governance as a theological issue. The complexity arises because questions of governance involve ontological, ethical, and political questions (i.e., questions of ultimate reality, questions of the good that ought to direct our actions, and questions of forms of government and social power). Questions of polity move us beyond practical concerns to concerns of basic outlook, beliefs, or value commitments.

2. Reflecting on "the congregational way."

Historically Unitarian Universalists have affirmed "the congregational way"—an imprecise designation, variously practiced in different denominational groups. *When we say we agree to govern ourselves in accordance with the principles of "congregational polity," we affirm the moral and spiritual values that we believe this form of governance expresses and sustains by its very nature.* Central among these values is the freedom of people to form self-determining, egalitarian, and democratic religious communities. If we are deeply committed to congregational polity, it is because its beliefs and values are central to our liberal faith.

Renewed discussion of congregational polity in terms of our basic values will deepen our commitment to practices that are shaped by a fuller appreciation of its meaning. For example, some may argue that the Department of Ministry can do a better job of matching ministers to congregations than a local congregation can, working independently. We would still object to such a system of centralized control, because congregational polity is not only an instrumental but also an intrinsic value. The role of the congregation in calling its own ministers is not merely a practical matter of achieving "a good fit" between minister and congregation. Deliberation on the kind of ministry a congregation wants and needs to fulfill its vision of itself brings into play the basic commitments of faith and value of the congregation. By generating and affirming such a vision a congregation constitutes itself as a dedicated community.

Furthermore, when it comes to affirming a particular individual as its minister, then "right relationship" is more important than abstract considerations like good fit. The process of covenanting, establishing a right relationship with a minister, goes to the heart of the spiritual enterprise. Congregations often complain of being misused by ministers, and ministers of being misused by congregations. These situations ask a prior question: Did they inadequately understand each other? Perhaps the church just thought they were hiring someone to preach things that pleased them, or perhaps the minister thought the "free pulpit" simply meant "you can do your own thing here." We need serious reflection and deliberation on what it means to be a community of faith and what it means to serve such a community.

These comments on the relationship between ministers and congregations illustrate the fact that the deepest theological issues are entailed in questions of our polity, our institutional practices.

3. Affirming the covenant among congregations.

Congregational polity is not, and could not be, the sole possession of any one congregation; in this sense, autonomy—being a law unto oneself—is a fiction. Congregational polity is itself a shared understanding, agreement, and commitment—in a word, a covenant—among various congregations; it presupposes their being in community and it furthers and sustains the actuality of that community.

We should recognize that it is difficult for us to give appropriate weight to this theological proposition, because we have only recently begun to regain a theological voice and vocabulary. The Principles of the UUA By-laws begin by saying "we covenant" but they do not speak of the covenanting congregations as corporate bodies. When subsequent passages of the By-laws explicitly mention congregational polity, it is not given positive significance—for example, as an agreement among member congregations to respect and support one another in the celebration and the living of their faith—but only negative significance in agreeing not to interfere with each other.

We need to affirm congregational polity as a covenant, that is, a mutual agreement and a commitment to walk together and support one another; it is an expression of our spiritual vision.

4. Embracing the church universal.

Congregational polity presupposes, then, some sense of loyalty and commitment to "the community of self-governing congregations." For Unitarian Universalists, this community is primarily embodied in the UUA; but because there are many Unitarian Universalist-related organizations and institutions not centrally organized under the UUA, the community is often spoken of as "the UU movement." But Unitarian Universalism or the UU movement are not the ultimate locus of our religious loyalty and commitment, because there are other religious bodies in North America and around the world with whom we also enjoy some sense of community. And beyond these organized religious bodies, there are myriad individuals, known and unknown, whom we would include in any full accounting of "the church universal."

> We need to affirm congregational polity as a covenant, a mutual agreement and a commitment to walk together and support one another.

This idea of the church universal is not limited to Christian groups. Some Unitarian Universalists would be surprised at the suggestion of a religious connection with anyone beyond the UU movement, if only because our preaching, pamphlets, and religious education have been predominantly sectarian. (For instance, we make virtually no attempt to teach children a sense of connection with the history of Christianity.) If we do not intend to suggest that ours is the only true religion, and all others are idolatries and superstitions, then we should affirm as much community with other religious bodies as we can.

Until recently a sectarian Unitarian Universalist emphasis has undercut our sense of having anything in common with other religious bodies; indeed, we have often defined ourselves by what we have rejected and stood against, usually orthodoxy. Some people have feared that if we lose this sectarian, oppositional edge, we will lose our reason for being. However, as we increasingly seek positive ways to define our faith, our sectarian stance may soften.

5. The congregation as a link between the individual and the universal religious community.

Any notion of the church universal, as affirmed by William Ellery Channing and other founders of the Unitarian Universalist tradition, is profoundly theological; it alters our understanding of the congregation (the local church). *The essential function of the congregation (the locally gathered, self-governing religious community) is to link the person to the universal religious community.* We may say that the congregation is the means by which we participate in what James Luther Adams called "the community-forming power."

The individual and the congregation need each other in the most fundamental way: For each to be fully itself, one needs to be in relationship with the other.

Through the congregation, the individual enables the universal religious community to become more than a nice idea; the individual enables it to become a historical reality. Conversely, through the congregation, the universal religious community calls the individual out of solitariness into solidarity with social, natural, and spiritual realities that transcend the self.

These statements *relativize* the congregation, in the sense of reminding us that our ultimate loyalty and commitment are not to "we few gathered here" or "our kind of people." At the same time, these statements *vitalize* the congregation by making explicit its basic reason for being, namely, its commitment to a spiritual ideal and to ends beyond itself (e.g., the community of love and justice). This may be called a prophetic vision of the church/congregation—the religious community not as an end in itself but as a bridge to a new community, a new humanity.

The individual and the congregation need each other in the most fundamental way: For each to be fully itself, one needs to be in relationship with the other.

6. **Enlarging the vision of the congregation.**
A new vision of congregational polity will view the congregation as the primary nexus of our spiritual life and ministry. When we understand the central mission of the congregation to be its corporate ministry (service) to the world, then the function of the UUA and other denominational organizations and institutions also becomes clear: to enable the congregations to carry out their ministries more effectively, both to their own constituencies (through congregation-directed services, for example) and to the world (through social action and humanitarian service, chaplaincies, theological education, publications, and the formation and renewal of congregations, for example).

A theological perspective (doctrine of the church) provides a basis for criticism and reform of both congregations and extra-congregational programs and groups. Two examples will clarify the critical function of theology.

- Racial and ethnic diversity becomes an important goal where there is commitment to a vision of the church as fully inclusive; such a vision exists in faith and hope before it can exist in reality, thus we call it theological. The religious community we believe in must represent the whole, glorious diversity of humanity.
- Community-based ministries will be fully supported only when congregations identify them as forms of our corporate ministry to the world, and community ministers are given professional roles within the congregations, including accountability, financial support, leading worship, and teaching.

Summary

As we increasingly accent the ideas of interdependence, relationship, and covenant in our self-interpretations, we will continue to build the theological groundwork for a fresh understanding of congregational polity—with emphasis on the community of self-governing congregations. As we move away from the ideal of rugged individualism on the personal level, we will also move away from it at the congregational level. This shift will have profound consequences for the ways in which we understand ministry, the meaning of membership, denominational and ecumenical relationships, the fundamental purpose and organizational form (covenant) of the congregation, and the vision of a universal spiritual community.

Recommendations

1. Students in the Unitarian Universalist ministry should engage in serious study of the theological dimensions of congregational life and polity.

2. The UUA should publish contemporary sermons, essays, books, and handbooks that promote broader and deeper reflection on the theology of religious community.

Sources

For critical review and suggestions regarding this section we are indebted to: Mark Belletini, minister of the Starr King Unitarian Church, Hayward, California; J. Ronald Engel, professor of social ethics, Meadville/Lombard Theological School, Chicago, Illinois; Earl Holt, minister of the First Unitarian Church, St. Louis, Missouri; Daniel Hotchkiss, UUA director for ministerial settlement, Boston, Massachusetts; Barbara Kiellor, president, Unitarian Universalist Process Theology Network, San Diego, California; Bruce Southworth, minister of the Community Church of New York, New York; and Conrad Wright, emeritus professor, Harvard Divinity School, Cambridge, Massachusetts.

References

Adams, James Luther, "Radical Laicism" and "The Enduring Validity of Congregational Polity," in *The Prophethood of All Believers*, ed. by George K. Beach (Boston: Beacon Press, 1986), pp. 93ff. and 127ff.

Barth, Joseph, *Toward a Doctrine of the Liberal Church* (Boston: The Minns Lectureship Committee, 1956).

Beach, George Kimmich, "The Dedicated Community," in *If Yes Is the Answer, What Is the Question?* (Boston: Skinner House Books, 1995), pp. 131-150.

The Free Church in a Changing World, Unitarian Universalist Association, 1963.

Foote, Henry Wilder, ed., *The Cambridge Platform of 1648, Tercentenary Commemoration at Cambridge, Massachusetts, October 27, 1948* (Boston: Beacon Press and Pilgrim Press, 1949).

Wright, Conrad, "A Doctrine of the Church for Liberals," in *Walking Together: Polity and Participation in Unitarian Universalist Churches* (Boston: Skinner House Books, 1989), pp. 1-24.

Wright, Conrad, "Congregational Polity and the Covenant." in *The Transient and the Permanent in Liberal Religion*, edited by Dan O'Neal, Alice Blair Wesley, and James Ishmael Ford (Boston: Skinner House Books, 1995), pp. 29-36.

SECTION TWO

Unitarian Universalist Tradition: A Short History

How did Unitarian Universalism become congregational? This section provides a brief history of the emergence of congregational polity in Unitarianism from its colonial roots and considers why these roots are still important to Unitarian Universalism. It also describes the evolution of American Universalism and notes the current practice of polity in the United States and Canada.

American Unitarianism came out of the congregational churches established in Massachusetts, which organized themselves around the principles articulated in the Cambridge Platform of 1648. This document was created to settle differences between local congregations on matters of church discipline and to explain themselves to the Church of England, to which they all professed to belong. Doctrinally consistent with the Reformation Christianity of the day, the Platform sought to prove that Congregationalism was the best and most biblically accurate form of church governance.

The Cambridge Platform holds that "there is no greater Church than a Congregation," which consists of visible saints in voluntary agreement and covenant with each other to "worship, edify and have fellowship."[1] Each church is autonomous, because there is no higher authority than the congregation. And yet the Platform also says:

> This government of the church is a mixed government. . . . In respect to Christ, the head and king of the church, it is a monarchy: In respect of the body, or Brotherhood of the church . . . it resembles a democracy. In

While discarding the doctrine of Lordship, have we also lost a principle of union? Are we in a community of congregations merely to simplify the delivery of services?

respect of the Presbyetry [sic] and power committed to them, it is an Aristocracy.²

Although the general description of the government of the church sounds foreign, some of the the details are familiar, such as granting members the right to determine their own leaders and standards of membership:

> In choosing their own officers, whether elders or deacons. In admission of their own members and therfore [sic], there is great reason they should have power to Remove any from their fellowship.

Congregational Polity Then and Now

Congregational polity then and now sees no power that extends beyond those who elected them, that is, a congregation. Then and now, a congregation has the right and responsibility to choose and ordain its own clergy, elect its own officers, direct them in the course of their duties, and replace them when necessary. Then and now there are no synods, bishops, or other persons empowered elsewhere with authority over a congregation.

However, some aspects of polity have changed over time. In addition to abandoning the principle of Lordship before Christ, we have also abandoned its earthly form, hierarchy, so that church officers are no longer understood to be models of Christ but delegates of the people. And few congregations maintain deacons. We have also left behind stringent requirements for membership, which in the colonial period meant a rigorous inquiry to ascertain the presence of grace and thus likely election to salvation. We count these changes as improvements. Yet we may not realize that we have also left behind the principle of intercongregational life. "Although Churches be distinct," the Platform reads, "and therefore may not be confounded one with another, and equal, and therefore have not Dominion one over another; yet all the Churches ought to preserve Church-Communion one with another, because they are all united unto Christ."³

While discarding the doctrine of Lordship, have we also lost a principle of union? Are we in a community of congregations merely to simplify the delivery of services? Does Unitarian Universalism have any meaning larger than what it means to any particular congregation?

If we choose to say that there is a connection among congregations, what would it be? The Cambridge Platform notes six duties that congregations owe to each other: care, consultation, admonition, participation, recommendation, and relief. The Platform also sanctions the calling of synods (or councils), official gatherings of congregations to settle general matters of dispute (such as that which created the Cambridge Platform).[4] None of these exists formally today. Those that exist informally are not uniform or consistent. These intercongregational duties are mainly absent from American Unitarian Universalism. How did that happen?

Congregational Polity in the American Unitarian Tradition

American Unitarianism emerged out of the culture that the Cambridge Platform described. Unitarian congregations elected their own leaders, determined their own membership (which was often how a congregation could be known as Unitarian), selected their own clergy, and paid their own way. The American Unitarian Association (organized in 1825 and succeeded by the Unitarian Universalist Association in 1961) mimicked the practice of synods and councils through its May meetings and fall meetings. The former were the business meetings of the Association, which was not (until much after 1825) composed of congregations. The latter were the occasions of debate on issues and matters of faith, suitable subjects for a true synod, but not binding.

Today we have the General Assembly, which continues the tradition of councils and synods, especially when revising the Bylaws. Lesser assemblies, local councils, exist at District meetings, but rarely do they take on the challenges of consulting, admonishing, and recommending. One of the few mutual duties we preserve is relief, as when congregations suffer catastrophic loss because of weather or fire. Very often individual congregations will respond with help. But perhaps there are other needs.

Conrad Wright, in his book *Walking Together,* has pointed out that, "congregationalism meant, and should still mean, not the autonomy of the local church, but the community of autonomous churches." That idea never existed in its ideal state, even in the years following the Cambridge Platform. In fact, the idea itself paled as change and controversy tested it. By 1720 there had been seven subsequent platforms and agreements, each compromising the standards set by the Cambridge Platform. Clearly, our recent experience rewriting the Bylaws is neither unique nor new.[5]

Between 1800 and 1825, New England congregationalism split into liberal and conservative wings. Churches divided over pulpit exchanges and ordinations. Councils that convened to settle disputes were torn apart by theological differences. So, too, were ministerial associations, which had come into existence early in New England, but were not officially a part of the polity. But they became the chief means by which churches connected and communicated.[6]

By 1825, the split was complete. The liberals formed the American Unitarian Association (AUA) and went their own way, organizing separate associations and institutions. Such organizing was itself a new phenomenon. In part it was the consequence of the new Massachusetts State Constitution, which dismantled government support for the congregational churches. Uncoupled from the state, religious bodies began to organize into independent bodies. The Unitarians, who doggedly protected congregational polity both as proof of their legitimacy and because it expressed early Unitarian ideals, found such organizing difficult. They even viewed the new denomination as anti-Unitarian and called it sectarianism. The most the Unitarians were willing to do was to develop a communication network through publications and the efforts of a secretary of the American Unitarian Association. There was, however, no formal structure that connected congregations; the AUA at that time was an organization of individuals rather than churches. The explicit belief that a congregation was by definition one among many receded.

The informal network remained intact, however, and was central to the Transcendentalist Controversy, which began when some ministers were accused of abandoning Christianity in favor of natural religion. The same tactics used by the conservative congregationals, such as shunning of colleagues, were used by Unitarians who disagreed with the likes of Ralph Waldo Emerson and Theodore Parker.

After the Civil War, during which some Unitarian clergy and congregations joined in relief efforts, an underlying structure for a congregational network formed through the creation of the National Conference of Unitarian Churches, which brought 200 Unitarian congregations into formal relationship with each other. In addition to regular meetings of the Conference on a national scale, numerous local conferences were also formed "for fellowship, consultation, and the framing of methods and plans for meeting the religious wants of their own allotted sphere."[7] The National Conference encouraged the understanding of congregational polity as a responsibility of churches for one another's welfare. Such an understanding was already at work in the semi-independent Western Unitarian Conference, thus the National Conference was especially effective there. In the west, the number of congregations doubled within a year.

By 1900, the Conference had matured into a strong body for advancing Unitarian institutional needs. In 1925 the American Unitarian Association and the National Conference (renamed the General Conference in 1911 to recognize the inclusion of Canadian members) were merged into a single body under the former's name. The AUA, which in 1884 began admitting church delegates to its meetings, had increasingly become the forum in which denominational policy and business matters were decided. The National Conference began to devote its energy to addressing theological and social issues. Under the new organization, business meetings were held annually in Boston, with biennial meetings, patterned after former Conference meetings, held elsewhere. It is difficult, though, to determine to what extent any "community of autonomous churches" emerged; we can presume wide variation from one geographical area to another. Wright points out that this centralization of power in the AUA was administrative, not ecclesiastical, in nature, and did not constitute a threat to the autonomy of the local church.

When the Great Depression began, the denomination began to decline, beset by problems of finances and leadership. By 1934 the situation had become so critical that a Commission of Appraisal was established to study the denomination and to make recommendations to strengthen it. That Commission, in its 1936 report, stated that "one of the most significant shifts in denominational organization during the present century has been the tendency away from decentralization toward centralization . . . with a corresponding dwindling of regional responsibility and activity." Such a dwindling, coupled with the weakened condition of the denomination, may have had an adverse effect on cooperative relationships among local churches and their sense of responsibility for each other.

While the American Unitarian Association underwent a dramatic renaissance from 1937 until 1958, decentralization did not take place. Whether decentralization would have promoted greater regional responsibility and stronger lateral relationships among churches is uncertain. Wright has pointed out that a decentralized structure does not necessarily strengthen such relationships; at least as crucial is the quality of communications taking place within the structure. Neither did growth in numbers change the culture of congregational individualism. Twenty-seven percent of all current congregations were organized between 1941 and the merger in 1961. If anything, there was even greater zeal for congregational individualism, perhaps to protect their freedom even from each other.[8]

Congregational Polity in the Universalist Tradition

In 1790, seventeen Universalists representing eight societies convened in Philadelphia, where they drew up articles of faith and an organizational plan. The plan of church government adopted by the delegates was described as "nearly that of the Congregational Church," and a church was defined as consisting "of a number of believers, united by covenant, for the purpose of maintaining the public worship of God, the preaching of the gospel, ordaining officers, preserving order and peace among its members, and relieving the poor." Each church was empowered to decide on the "call, qualifications, and gifts, of those who wish to devote themselves to God and the ministry," and to "solemnly set apart and ordain such persons." Not only were ministers to be ordained, but also deacons, who

Someone once said the Universalists were organized like Presbyterians and acted like Congregationalists; Unitarians were organized like Congregationalists and acted like Presbyterians.

were "to attend to the secular affairs of the church." No ordinances were to be insisted on as obligatory, and "all such persons who hold the articles of faith and maintain good works" should be admitted into church membership. In addition, "the communion of the churches" was to be accomplished by a "convention of the churches held annually by deputies or messengers, to inquire into, and report, the state of each church . . . and to send forth ministers to propagate the gospel." Finally, it was made clear that all the actions of the Convention would "be issued only by way of advice or recommendation."[9]

Four years later, the New England Convention of Universalists, meeting in Oxford, Massachusetts, "adopted the Philadelphia platform of articles of faith and form of church government, and recommended that the same be observed by the churches and societies forming this Convention." In the words of Richard Eddy, a nineteenth-century Universalist historian, "So far as recommendations could effect it, this action of the Convention brought all the Universalists of the land into harmony of belief in regard to the great essentials of doctrine, and was an emphatic endorsement of organization and discipline."[10] In using the phrase "all the Universalists of the land," Eddy was reasonably accurate: The Philadelphia and New England Conventions included most Universalist churches then in existence, probably about fifty in number. The New England Convention evolved into the General Convention of Universalists.

The organizational plan adopted by the two conventions closely resembles that of New England congregationalism of the same period. By 1803, however, when the New England Convention met in Winchester, New Hampshire, it was evident that the articles of faith and plan of church government adopted earlier did not anticipate the growing movement's diversity of faith and practice. As a result, the delegates adopted a simplified and liberalized profession of belief, with a liberty clause forbidding a congregation or association from requiring a creedal test or other conformity to certain statements of belief. The delegates also adopted an organizational plan that allowed latitude at the local level while strengthening the Convention's powers with regard to discipline, fellowship, and ordination. The plan also recommended formation of "associations" of congregations within the Convention. In organizing associations within a convention, the Universalists were following the practice of the Baptists; this is not surprising, because many Universalists had come from Baptist congregations.

As the Universalist movement grew, conventions organized in each New England state and several others. A four-layer pyramidal structure emerged, with the General Convention at the top, descending to state conventions, local associations, and at the base, local societies. Most decisions about discipline, fellowship, and ordination were made at the state level, although for a time this power was shared with the associations. (This concentration of power in the state conventions persisted until the merger with the Unitarians in 1961.)

When the Unitarian Controversy ended in the mid-1830s, the two denominations were operating under quite different organizational plans. During the years leading up to the Universalist Centennial in 1870, repeated attempts were made to strengthen denominational structure in general and the General Convention in particular. A period of rapid growth was coming to an end and feeling was widespread that the denomination needed tighter organization and consolidation of its gains. A "Report on the State of the Church" made to the 1858 General Convention stated that "our organization is sadly defective, approaching far more nearly to no organization at all, than to an official denominational unity." Some people argued that the denomination should end the pretense of having a centralized structure and return to a purely congregational polity. A report in 1860 replied, "Whatever be the wishes and predilections of individuals among us, our general policy is not Congregational. The fathers . . . voluntarily departed from Congregational usages many years ago, and adopted the general principles that everywhere mark our polity. A return to Congregationalism, even if desirable, is doubtless impractical." Conrad Wright notes that "this is not as anti-congregational as it may seem, since what is understood here by congregationalism is the isolated autonomy of the local church"; moreover, Universalist churches had always selected their ministers and managed their internal affairs.

In 1865, a new constitution for the General Convention was adopted that asserted the General Convention's jurisdiction over state conventions in matters of discipline and fellowship and established salaried offices. In addition, the General Convention was incorporated, permitting it to collect and disperse funds. Five years later, at the Centennial Sessions at Gloucester, Massachusettes, yet another constitution was adopted in an attempt to strengthen the authority of the General Convention. Local associations were eliminated as an official part of the denominational structure and the liberty clause was removed from the Winchester Profession of Faith. Henceforth all ministers were required to subscribe to the Winchester Profession to retain fellowship, limiting the power of a local church in its choice of minister. The liberty clause was reinstated with the Boston Declaration of 1899, but the loss of the associations was permanent.

The period between the world wars was difficult for Universalism. Organizationally, Universalists were suspicious of centralized power, which made it difficult to mount any unified action. Sociologically, the migration to the cities and the west left many town and village churches without enough members to sustain them. And theologically, the uniqueness of the movement was undermined as the mainline denominations approached a more liberal view on damnation, which had historically separated Universalists from other Christians. By the mid-1930s, Universalists, like their Unitarian cousins, were weak and in disarray.

Fortunately, like the Unitarians, the Universalists found vital new leadership. To promote a clearer denominational identity, they successfully changed their name from the Universalist General Convention to the Universalist Church of America (UCA). They also adopted a new vision of what Universalism should be in the modern world: an uncircumscribed church that would welcome "theist and humanist, unitarian and trinitarian, colored and colorless." Superintendent Robert Cummins repudiated isolationism and called for denominational unity:

> A local parish *is* The Universalist Church finding expression and taking form in a given locality. It is *not* an independent body; nor is it merely a part or segment of the Church as a whole. It is the whole of The Universalist Church coming to focus within a particular group of Universalists at a particular place.[11]

In a real sense Cummins was articulating the reason for the "communion of the churches" that the Universalists in Philadelphia had called for 150 years earlier. Even more, this statement is among the best expressions of why congregational polity is not atomistic and independent.

Before the merger, Universalist churches were governed by a polity that was partly congregational and partly presbyterian. Churches chose their own ministers and controlled their internal affairs, finances, and property; in their ongoing life they were largely autonomous. Ordination and fellowshipping were directed by the state conventions and, in some instances, by the Universalist Church of America itself. It appears that "the communion of the churches" was far from real within the denomination, although sometimes approached at the state convention level.

Gordon McKeeman, a Unitarian Universalist cleric with strong Universalist roots, offered the following description of the two merging movements: "Someone once said in commenting on the difference between Unitarian and Universalist polities that the Universalists were organized like Presbyterians and acted like Congregationalists; Unitarians were organized like Congregationalists and acted like Presbyterians."[12] This comment points to something beyond official policy, namely, culture. The ambiance attributed to Universalism, gentleness and kindness, made the Presbyterian form of organization acceptable, since it did not intrude in local affairs. Among Unitarians, Congregationalism was experienced as cool and shrewd, a means to preserve identity and pursue one's interests. These are stereotypes, certainly, but supported by enough anecdotal evidence to make them at least occasionally true.

Congregational Polity in the Unitarian Universalist Tradition

The Constitution and Bylaws adopted by the Unitarian Universalist Association in 1961 reflect a clear choice of the Unitarian model as the Association's guiding principle of governance. Article II, Section 3, affirmed "the independence and autonomy of local churches, fellowships and associate members"; and that "nothing in this Constitution or Bylaws of the Association shall be deemed to infringe upon the congregational polity of churches and fellowships." Although the wording has been changed over the years, the current 1994 Bylaws continue to affirm congregational polity.

After the merger, six study commissions were organized under the heading "The Free Church in a Changing World." The first of these commissions considered the issue of congregational polity in its work. An interim report cited similarities between the two denominations on the three basic principles of congregational polity: both hold that the final authority lies with the individual, both hold to the essential autonomy of the local church, and both hold to the necessity for autonomous churches to come together in free association. These are the principles on which we now unite.

The report further suggested that

> "congregational polity," like "freedom" and "democracy," is often a stop thought device for us and warned that we must pay sharper attention whenever the phrase is invoked. The principle should frequently be stated. But the practice must be tested by the principle.[13]

The final 1963 report replaced the previous statements with vaguer language and less emphasis on historical background. The report spelled out four explicit rights reserved to the local church: the right to admit members in accordance with its own definition of membership, the right to select its own leadership, the right to control its own property, and the right to enter freely and voluntarily into association with other churches. In addition, the principles underlying congregational polity were restated:

1. That a local congregation is a complete church with all the powers of a church;
2. That its being and powers rest upon the free, deliberate consent of the individual members; and
3. That all business shall be conducted within the church in accordance with accepted rules of order.[14]

The right of the local church to admit members in accordance with its own definition of membership was challenged almost at once. At the 1963

We continue to struggle to create a more effective association by trying to ameliorate the most frustrating features of an association.

General Assembly in Chicago a constitutional amendment was proposed to require maintenance of open membership by churches and fellowships as a qualification for voting rights in the General Assembly, a move to ensure that Blacks would not be discriminated against. After an emotional debate the proposal was defeated, failing to receive the necessary two-thirds vote. Those opposing the amendment, although as firmly opposed to discrimination as those supporting it, argued that the method proposed for achieving open membership was unworkable and represented an infringement on congregational polity.[15] In subsequent years the Bylaws were amended to affirm the Association's "special responsibility and that of its member societies and organizations, to promote the full participation of persons . . . without regard to race, color, sex, disability, affectional or sexual orientation, age or national origin."[16] However, as Dr. McKeeman commented:

> the efforts to provide fair access to pulpits to women, to homosexuals, to the handicapped has proceeded on the philosophical notion that belonging to the UUA commits local churches to such an effort. But the Association's Bylaws clearly provide that nothing in the Bylaws shall infringe upon the freedom of the local congregation. So we continue to struggle to create a more effective association by trying to ameliorate the most frustrating features of an association.[17]

Current Practice

A congregation may legally act as it wishes, but is such action consonant with the Principles and Purposes that define the community of congregations?

Tensions between the Association and the local congregation have been felt in recent years as well. The composition of the Board of Trustees, originally elected entirely at large, has been altered so that the majority are elected from districts. Doubtless intended to ensure broader representation by region, the change made districts more significant. The trustees and president are allowed to speak for the Association on social matters without direction from the congregations. Finances of the Association are entirely controlled by the trustees. The Department of Ministry at one time suggested withholding ordination certificates to those accepting ordination before being Fellowshipped. Congregations lack choice (other than refusal) in the placement of extension ministers. These practices, although technically permissible, nonetheless tread upon the perceived liberties of the congregation.

Other policies and practices emphasize local autonomy. Congregations can ordain at their discretion, whether or not the ordinand is acceptable to other clergy or congregations.[18] When a congregation has clearly failed to uphold both the Principles of the Association and its basic rules, the

26 Congregational Polity in Theory and Practice

rights of the congregation are at odds with the interests of the Association. A congregation may legally act as it wishes, but is such action consonant with the Principles and Purposes that define the community of congregations?

There is also a variety of experiments that may enhance the community of autonomous churches. Some are old, like The Benevolent Fraternity, which was organized by Boston-area Unitarian societies 175 years ago. Member congregations jointly support a community ministry serving the Boston area. More recently, the North Texas Area Unitarian Universalist Societies have for some years shared responsibility for a large housing development. Congregations in Minnesota's Twin Cities area have created a common coming of age program for their youth. More than twenty years ago the Association sponsored a Renewal in Growth program, which paired congregations in mutual assessment and advice. For many people in our congregations, groups such as the Unitarian Universalist Women's Federation, the Unitarian Universalist Christian Fellowship, or the Unitarian Universalist Service Committee serve to broaden identity and knit commitments to Unitarian Universalism.

Summary

Thoughout their once separate and now joint experience, Unitarian Universalists have struggled with the ideals of autonomy and community. Unitarians, in particular, chose to err on the side of autonomy, refusing even to become a community of congregations for most of their first century. Universalists were more willing to create communities of congregations, yet even they understood each congregation to be the chief center of religious life.

Each community was also impoverished by the isolation of congregations from each other. Each made attempts to be more cohesive. Each saw a measure of success and failure, and wrestled with resistance.

However, the ideal existed before the actual: The vision of the Cambridge Platform of a devoted community of congregations came into being before many congregations were formed. It governed the aspirations of those who wrote the Platform and those who succeeded them, and it is still an ideal that Unitarian Universalism embraces.

References

The Free Church in a Changing World (Boston: Unitarian Universalist Association), Interim Report, no date; Final Report, 1963.

Charles Howe, "He Lives Tomorrow: Clinton Lee Scott, Revitalizer of Universalism," *Proceedings of the Unitarian Universalist Historical Society,* Vol. XXI, Part II.

Russell E. Miller, *The Larger Hope*, Vols. I and II (Boston: UUA, 1979, 1985).

Unitarian Universalist Register-Leader (Boston: Unitarian Universalist Association).

Notes

1. Williston Walker, *Creeds and Platforms of Congregationalism* (Philadelphia: Pilgrim Press, 1989), pp. 207, 209.
2. *Ibid.*, pp. 217-218.
3. *Ibid.*, pp. 230 233.
4. *Ibid.*, pp 233-234.
5. After the Cambridge Platform of 1648 came the Half Way Covenant of 1657, the Savoy Declaration of 1658, the "Reforming Synod" of 1679, the "Heads of Agreement" of 1691, the Proposals of 1705, and the Saybrook Platform of 1708. Another four documents followed by 1883.
6. Walker, *Creeds and Platforms of Congregationalism,* p. 461. Ministerial associations were recognized as part of the legitimate structure of congregationalism by The Heads of Agreement written in Boston, 1691.
7. Earl Morse Wilbur, *A History of Unitarianism in Transylvania, England, and America* (Boston: Beacon Press, 1945), pp. 470 ff.; Conrad Wright, *op. cit.*; and conversations with the Commission.
8. Conrad Wright, "Congregational Polity as Practiced by the Unitarians and the Universalists: A Historical Survey," work in progress, 1995. Centralism may be abetted by congregational individualism. Individual congregations cannot provide for all their needs, notably settling new clergy. Informal structures existed from colonial times, when candidates were most often new graduates recommended by the faculty to local congregations. Ministerial associations served to assure soundness of doctrine and character. Later, denominational leaders often exerted a significant influence on the settlement process.
9. Richard Eddy, *Universalism in America, Vol. 1* (Boston: Universalist Publishing House, 1884), pp. 296-302.
10. *Ibid.*, p. 432.
11. Robert Cummins, *Parish Practice in Universalist Churches* (Boston: Murray Press, 1946), pp. 41-42.

12. Gordon McKeeman, in "Polity Among Unitarians and Universalists," edited by Peter Raible, 1992, unpublished, pp. 1339-1340.
13. Charles Howe, "He Lives Tomorrow: Clinton Lee Scott, Revitalizer of Universalism," *Proceedings of the Unitarian Universalist Historical Society,* Vol. XXI, Part II.
14. *The Free Church in a Changing World* (Boston: Unitarian Universalist Association), Interim Report, no date; Final Report, 1963.
15. *Unitarian Universalist Register-Leader,* Mid-summer, 1963, pp. 10-12.
16. UUA Bylaws, 1994, Article III, Sections: C-2.3.
17. McKeeman, *Polity Among Unitarians and Universalists,* p. 1339.
18. *Ibid.,* pp. 1340-1341.

SECTION THREE

Comparative Congregationalisms

Unitarian Universalists are not unique; other religious bodies have also found congregational polity to be consonant with their values. Nor are all Unitarians and Universalists congregational. This section describes three non-Unitarian Universalist congregational groups and two non-congregational Unitarian and Universalist groups to provide insight into the relationship between our faith and its form.

Congregationalisms abound. In addition to Congregationalists themselves (the United Church of Christ), all variety of Baptists, the Disciples of Christ, Mennonites, Quakers, and Jews are congregational. Interviews with Presbyterian and Episcopal clergy indicate that an informal congregationalism exists even in these denominations.

First, we will examine two non-Unitarian Universalist denominations that are close to our experience: the United Church of Christ (to which we are related historically) and the American Baptist Convention. Then we will consider the Union of American Hebrew Congregations, with whom we share very little in tradition or premise.

We then consider two examples of non-congregational Unitarianism and Universalism: the Unitarian Church in Transylvania, which has bishops and elders, and the Universalist Church of the Philippines, which has a unique meta-congregationalism. Contemplating alternative forms of our common faith may reveal new possibilities for congregational life.

Culture is a strong influence on the form of polity that a denomination takes.

The United Church of Christ

In contrast to the Unitarian Universalist Association, the United Church of Christ conferences have more influence over local church life because they are the agencies of church and clergy standing.

Until the creation of the American Unitarian Association, we shared a common history with the Congregationalists. The Cambridge Platform of 1648 is the constitutional document of congregationalism, both Trinitarian and Unitarian:

> The Platform interpreted the church catholic as all those who are elected and called to salvation. A "militant visible church on earth" was understood to exist in particular congregations as "a company of saints by calling, united into one body, by a holy covenant for the public worship of God and the mutual edification of one another." Christ was the head of the church; the congregation, independent of outside interference, had the right to choose its own officials. The office of the civil magistrate was subject to recognition by the church. Churches were to preserve communion with one another in mutual covenant with Christ.[1]

During the early nineteenth century, Congregational churches were moved by controversy with the liberals (now Unitarians) to create a new college to ensure sound doctrinal education. This school, Andover-Newton Theological, was their first shared endeavor. In 1810, the faculty of Andover and the Massachusetts General Association authorized a mission effort, leading to the formation of the American Board of Commissioners for Foreign Missions, chartered by the government in 1812. Similar efforts took place in the German Reformed Church both abroad and domestically. These became the agencies for growing denominationalism, as state and local organizations were unable to mount missionary work as effectively as a large group. The first national Congregational organization emerged in 1852.[2]

The present-day United Church of Christ (UCC) describes itself as a "united and uniting church," comprised of two bodies that were themselves formed from others. One united the colonial Congregationalism of Puritan ancestry with the Christian Church (which helped established Meadville Theological School with the Unitarians). The two became the Congregational Christian Churches in 1931. The other was the Evangelical and Reformed Church, formed in 1934 from two German and Swiss Reformed churches dating back to colonial days. The Congregational Christian Churches and the Evangelical and Reformed Church united in 1957.[3] Today's UCC includes the Board of Homeland Ministries, which was established by the Congregationalists before merger and has responsibility for domestic missions and education. The UCC also includes the Board of World Ministries, the descendent of the American Board of Commissioners for Foreign Missions.

The structure of the UCC consists of local churches organized into area bodies, which coordinate programs and services. These also administer church and clergy standing, which determine whether a congregation or clergyperson is recognized by other churches and clergy. For example, an Ecclesiastical Council composed of clergy and laity from churches in the local association examines candidates for the pastorate. To be in good standing, the candidate must submit to this examination, approval of which is necessary for a recognized ordination. The congregation may choose not to follow these rules, but doing so means the minister would not be recognized as having standing among other UCC churches.

The General Synod, the representative body of the UCC, is composed of church members elected by the conferences. The Synod meets biennially and elects general officers and most of the Executive Council, which functions as a board of trustees.

Each congregation is guaranteed local autonomy. In contrast to the Unitarian Universalist Association, the United Church of Christ associations and groups of associations, called conferences, have much more influence over local church life because they are the agencies of church and clergy standing.

American Baptist Churches

The Baptist tradition in the United States began with Roger Williams's removal from Massachusetts to Rhode Island and developed with the rise of local associations of Baptist churches, especially the Philadelphia Association of 1707. This group, known as Particular Baptists, is the parent of current Baptist organizations in the United States.

The Philadelphia Association shared the opinion of the first English Baptists (c. 1650) that "Though we be distinct in respect of our particular bodies ... yet are all one in communion, holding Jesus Christ to be our head and Lord." Elsewhere it was said that "There is the same relationshipe betwixt particular churches towards each other, as there is betwixt particular members of one church."[4] Thus the Association would, like a congregation, have the power to include or exclude a church, as a church may choose to accept or deny someone membership. Because the Baptists placed a high theological premium on being in association, owing to the belief that the church universal was larger than any single church, the power of the association was considerable.

In addition to maintaining spiritual discipline, the Association was charged with edifying the membership, creating new churches, providing and ensuring suitable clergy, and settling disputes between churches. As membership grew, additional associations began to perform these local functions. These associations, in turn, sought to maintain fellowship with each other, so strong was the conviction that piety required community.

Following the independence of the United States, the local associations were overcome by the rise of state conventions (state-level associations) and independent groups that served special interests. In addition, the stresses of national growth and controversy enhanced the sense of independence of local Baptist churches. By the beginning of the twentieth century, Baptist churches were known for their rugged individualism. Associational life became all but a memory.

On the question of polity the American Baptist Churches (ABC) continues to be vigilant about protecting local autonomy. Like the UUA, the ABC has a proliferation of societies and other independent agencies to promote education, mission, and other causes. The presence of state conventions resembles Universalist practices before merger.

Like the United Church of Christ, the ABC considers its General Board to be a representative body composed of members elected by districts, similar to associations. These districts have between 40 and 60 churches within them, and may contain regional, state, or city groupings (sometimes called RSCs) that existed before the organization of the ABC.

While governance is by election district, services are rendered through regional, state, and city groupings. As in the UCC, executive ministers serve both denominational and congregational needs (somewhat like Unitarian Universalist field staff).

As in the UCC, the ABC's practice of ordination entails much greater area involvement than in the UUA. Local congregations must license candidates for the ministry through committees set up for that purpose. Like the UCC, an ecclesiastical council (called a Council of Ordination) is required, but it may be identical to the local Department of Ministry for the region, state, or city. Ordinations that take place without approval of the council are considered unilateral and without standing.

The Union of American Hebrew Congregations

Ten people of Jewish faith can form a congregation and legitimately call themselves a synagogue. Forming a Unitarian Universalist congregation is much more complicated.

Rabbi Isaac Meyer Wise came to the United States in 1846, in part to create a reform movement in Judaism. Efforts to accomplish this goal in Europe had not succeeded, at least in part because of the resistance of the Orthodox and the suspicions of national authorities. In 1873 Wise united 34 congregations into the Union of American Hebrew Congregations (UAHC). The principles behind this organization were general: to encourage and organize Jewish congregations, to promote education and enrich Jewish life, and to foster activities that perpetuate and advance Judaism.

In 1873, Hebrew Union College opened to train indigenous rabbis for the new reform movement. Later the Union would expand its role to include maintaining the Hebrew Union College, strengthening the solidarity of Jewish people, fostering development of liberal Judaism, and strengthening the state of Israel. Wise subsequently organized the Central Conference of American Rabbis (CCAR) in 1889 as the clerical arm of Reform Judaism.

Congregational life and purpose differ between Jewish and Christian religions. For example, the constitution of the UAHC, in describing its membership, says, "Any Jewish congregation . . . upon approval of the Board of Trustees may become a member of the Union by subscribing to its constitution and bylaws."[5] Although the Union encourages and supports the growth of new congregations, they originate without such help. In contrast, Unitarian Universalist congregations cannot exist without the initial involvement of the UUA. Ten people of Jewish faith can form a congregation and legitimately call themselves a synagogue. Forming a Unitarian Universalist congregation is much more complicated.

The Union preserves congregational autonomy in its constitution, as does the UUA. A General Assembly and board of trustees play the same general role as in the UUA, but the powers and relations between them are quite different. Here are some examples:

- Membership is financial and failure to contribute is grounds for removal. Dues are levied as a percentage of operating expenses. Congregations are expected to file a detailed report of their annual income and expenses. A mechanism for adjusting the amount is reserved only for special cases by request.
- The board of trustees numbers more than 220 members, with 50 percent elected from regional associations, called councils, much like UUA districts. However, each council has more than one trustee; the exact number depends on the size of the council. Each council delegation selects its own president. The rest of the board is made up of officers of the Union, officers of the CCAR, presidents of national affiliates, two officers of the Hebrew Union College, and a number of at-large trustees elected by the General Assembly.
- The chair of the board is the Chief Executive Officer of the Union, and is elected by the board, not the General Assembly. The president is appointed by the board and serves at its pleasure.
- The board alone has the authority to create affiliates, which when recognized have a seat on the board. However, the chair and the president of the Union must be members of the affiliate's executive committee.

It is clear that the UAHC sees its board as a governing body. And by reserving election of officers to the board itself, it also asserts a corporate model of power. By having more trustees, member congregations have greater access to their board than do Unitarian Universalist congregations, even though the board retains discretionary authority. Like the UUA, the power of the purse resides in the board.

It is also clear that associational life is congregational life writ large. For example, Jewish congregations entrust to their board full authority, including the power to hire and fire rabbis. Likewise, the board of the UAHC names the president. There seems to be a higher value placed on ensuring effective power than on preventing abuses of power. Likewise, exacting dues from member congregations resembles the practice of assessing dues of individual synagogue members.

In the UUA, by contrast, congregations elect the president separately from the board, and habitually invest the office in a clergyperson, much as a congregation chooses a board but reserves the power to name its clergy. Power is more divided, perhaps because it is more suspect. Finances are considered voluntary and setting dues is anathema. At most, a congregation can set minimums and suggest higher levels.

Another marked difference is the role of the clergy. Reform rabbis are trained and ordained by the Hebrew Union College-Jewish Institute of Religion. Rabbinic authority resides in the school, not in the congregation, but the UAHC controls the board of the school.

Rabbis have a different role in the congregation than in UU or other Christian congregational associations. They have voting rights on the board of their congregation, and they have representation as a body as well as individually on the Union board. Compared with UU tradition and practice, there is more conscious equality between clergy and laity in Reform Judaism, which can be both liberating and troublesome. Friction between board and rabbi is almost a cliché and congregational challenges to the board are commonplace.

Common Aspects Across Congregationalisms

For the UUA the question is whether we have a vision that makes associating worth the effort and cost.

All three denominations—the United Church of Christ, the American Baptist Convention, and the Union of American Hebrew Congregations—formed strong associations to further their purposes. For the UCC, missionary work was the initial reason for association. The biblical mandate to share the gospel drove independent congregations into league with one another. Among the Baptists, missionary work was again the impetus to association. But like the UUA, resistance to control and inwardness have limited associational unity. In the UAHC, the need for a community of liberal Jews and for a sympathetic rabbinate have encouraged interdependence.

For the UUA the question is whether we have a vision that makes associating worth the effort and cost. This question is pertinent to the Association, but also inhabits the local congregation.

The Unitarian Church of Transylvania

The oldest Unitarian organization in existence is also the most complex. In the region bounded by Catholic Hungary to the west, Protestant portions of Bohemia and Poland to the north, Ottoman Muslims on the east and Orthodox Greeks and Slavs to the northeast and south, Transylvania gave rise to a Unitarian polity more akin to Lutheranism and Presbyterianism than congregationalism.

The most influential force, though, has been the state. Throughout most of its 500-year history, Transylvanian Unitarianism has been either controlled or suppressed by the government. Before and after the Ceausescu regime, the government was biased toward an Eastern Orthodox model of the church and its relation to the state. Unitarianism was thus both in a theological and an ecclesiastical minority. Under various regimes, from the Austro-Hungarian Empire to Communism, Unitarianism was enjoined to follow strict rules that prevented changes, owing to a law that dates to the sixteenth century. Today, church buildings and contents are owned by the state. All changes must still be approved by the Department of Cults. Radical change has long been dangerous.

Authority in the Unitarian Church of Transylvania is vested in the Consistory, which is made up of lay-people and clergy from church districts in Transylvania. The lay president of the consistory is also lay president of the Unitarian Church at large. Local churches elect lay members of Consistory.

A bishop is elected by the Consistory, which meets quarterly. The bishop, who has always been male and a clergyman previously served a life term. Under new bylaws, the bishop is elected to a six-year term. The bishop is very powerful both as the executive power of the Consistory and, by serving for many years, as the most senior and experienced member of the Consistory itself. An annual General Assembly of elected laypeople meets in December. An Executive Committee also works with the bishop.

The bishop's responsibilities include appointing clergy to smaller churches and consulting with larger churches searching for clergy; administering the church at large, controlling denominational funds, and managing church property. Before World War I, the bishop had absolute control of church property and its use. The bishop controls parochial high schools and colleges (including the seminary), and supervises all church personnel, including the deans, who are executive ministers of the five districts. These deans are elected by local clergy but work with and for the bishop. The dean has pastoral oversight of local clergy, and runs district meetings.

Church membership is determined at birth by parentage (boys are assigned to the father's faith, girls to the mother's) and changing churches is rare. Before 1989, the Communist culture discouraged attachment either

Throughout most of its 500-year history, Transylvanian Unitarianism has been either controlled or suppressed by the government.

to a religion or a local church, but the new regime offers less hostility to religion and thus sparks more interest.

Local churches have a lay board, elected annually, with a lay president and lay treasurer. In smaller towns the bell ringer is also an office of significance, as the church bell is also the town clock. The minister relates to the board as the bishop to the Consistory. In reality and symbolically, the pastor is the most powerful person in the church. In smaller parishes, the pastor also functions informally as the village mayor and elder.

An episcopal form of polity governs the Unitarian Church in Transylvania. True to episcopacy, the bishop has power over the appointment of clergy, the disposition of certain property, and the supervision of regional executives. A Presbyterian form of polity is also at work, as the bishop is elected by a Consistory, not elevated by other bishops, and the deans are elected by the clergy. Congregational power is limited by the power of the bishop and the dean, but especially by the state. None of the customary measures of congregationalism applies: Members do not own their property, select their members, control their finances, select their clergy, or determine whether to be in association. The only power the lay government seems to have is the election of local officers, and their authority seems very limited.

How the polity of the Transylvanian Unitarian Church operates in fact is much harder to say. Knowledgeable sources affirm the power of the bishop and the extended power of the clergy. The influence that the laity has over their clergy, and the Consistory and General Assembly over the bishop, may be subtle but real. But our information suggests that this model is far from the congregational polity of the UUA.

The Universalist Church of the Philippines

In 1991, the UUA admitted the Universalist Church of the Philippines into membership amid much controversy. Its founder, the Reverend Jorge Quimada, was murdered in 1992 in a political assassination. The church dates from an April 1955 meeting organized and led by the Reverend Quimada. The UUA had never before admitted a congregation of non-North American origin and culture. These and other issues are all invoked by that action, among them the collision of polities.

The Unitarian Universalist Church of the Philippines is a collection of 17 congregations, mostly lay-led fellowship-style groups. They choose leaders, establish rules, collect money, and spend it. Some have erected buildings from their own funds; others rent or borrow meeting places. Each congregation determines the rules for membership.

A convention of delegates from each of the 17 congregations meets annually. Before UUA affiliation there was one executive minister in a lifetime position, the Reverend Quimada, and none since his death. Other ministers work for the congregations. It is not clear whether they are itinerant or settled, but all were licensed by the Reverend Quimada.

This bare outline will be amplified when a complete account is written by Rebecca Sienes, the Reverend Quimada's daughter and the source for this material, but sufficient information exists to establish that the Unitarian Universalist Church of the Philippines is not congregational by North American standards. While local groups are largely self-governing, professional leadership is almost independent of the lay portion of the polity. The Reverend Quimada made his position very powerful, especially in the licensing of ministers. What is unknown is how the local congregations related to the executive minister, individually and collectively. Other questions remain unanswered. What is the role of the Convention? How are congregations formed? Are clergy paid and by whom? For whom do they work?

Summary

Culture is a strong influence on the form of polity that a denomination takes. The Transylvanian Unitarian Church is clearly a product of its history, being trapped by circumstances in a form that has not been allowed to change for more than 500 years. The Unitarian Universalist Church of the Philippines, spread throughout an archipelago, may have established a meta-congregation largely to overcome geographical isolation. Where interconnection and collaboration are inherently difficult because of physical and cultural conditions, a central clergyperson may provide needed unity and stability.

Likewise, the great variety of congregationalisms in the United States and Canada, covering all manner of denominations may also be a product of North American culture. The extensive research on voluntary associations by James Luther Adams, to say nothing of the insights of de Toqueville and William James, suggest that it is hard to be non-congregational in the United States. Functional congregationalism pervades Episcopalianism and Presbyterianism and even aspects of the Roman Catholic Church. Only other-worldly sects, those that reject the culture, seem to have escaped the tendency toward congregationalism. Unitarian Universalists are congregational for more than ideological or Unitarian Universalist reasons. See Section 5, "The Spiritual and Culural Ethos of Unitarian Universalism," for an exploration of how our polity reflects aspects of our cultural identity.

These comparisons raise a number of questions: Are there choices in the wide assortment of congregationalisms that may be more useful in accomplishing our goals? Should we form associations like the UCC and vest each with Fellowship Committee powers? Should we require ecclesiastical councils to involve several congregations in calling and ordaining ministers? Should we focus the Association itself on more external goals (education and mission) and less on institutional maintenance? These goals have served the Baptists and Jews very well. Shall we link our governing boards as the Union of American Hebrew Congregations does, or make seminaries (with associational influence) the guardians of clerical qualifications?

The Unitarian Church of Transylvania and the Universalist Church of the Philippines provide two models of the ability to be a faithful Unitarian or Universalist in non-congregational ways. This serves notice that there is no one vessel adequate to a particular theology, even ours. To see that other models exist and work passably well is a lesson in humility for our culture. And while each model has its own drawbacks, we have ours as well.

Sources

Material for this section was gathered from interviews with the following people: E. Nils Blatz, rector of Grace Church Episcopal, Brooklyn, New York; Leslie Dobbs-Alsopp, associate pastor, First Presbyterian, Brooklyn, New York; May Mass, regional administrator, New York Federation of Reform Synagogues; Richard Beal, Unitarian Universalist minister, Louisville, Kentucky; Kenneth Torquil MacLean, Unitarian Universalist Association International Liaison; Rebecca Sienes, student at Meadville Theological School, member of the Unitarian Universalist Church of the Philippines, and daughter of the late Reverend Quimada; and Helen Backhouse, Canadian Unitarian Council member and former member of the Commission on Appraisal.

Notes

1. *History and Program, United Church of Christ* (Cleveland: United Church Press, 1986, 1991), p. 15.
2. *Ibid.*, p. 23-24.
3. *Ibid.*, p. 5-6, 29-30.
4. *A Baptist Manual of Polity and Practice,* p. 150.
5. *Constitution and Bylaws of the UAHC, as amended October 1993* (New York: UAHC Press), p. 5.

SECTION FOUR

The UUA Bylaws: A Study in Ambivalence

The UUA Bylaws (adopted in 1961 and amended since) are a basic document of our community of autonomous churches. Like the founding charter of any community, this document reflects the original vision of the community. It also reflects in the history of its amendments the previously unclarified and unresolved issues that the community has sought to resolve. Many provisions of Articles II and III of the UUA Bylaws bear upon our understanding of congregational polity. The Bylaws reveal a deeply ambivalent attitude toward our congregational heritage. This section reviews the UUA Bylaws as they relate to our understanding of congregational polity to clarify how we can evolve toward a "more perfect union"—one in which the Association energizes its member congregations and the congregations in turn energize the Association.

As a principle of governance, congregational polity figures significantly in the first articles of the Bylaws of the Unitarian Universalist Association. The Bylaws define the purposes of the Association and the ways in which its constituent member groups—primarily its congregations—relate to the UUA. We often speak of "unity in diversity" in terms of how individual members relate to their church or fellowship. But we also view unity in diversity as the ideal relationship between the UUA and a congregation. A close reading of the UUA Bylaws reveals the extent to which the two sides of this equation—unity and diversity—are in tension with each other. Sometimes we accent our shared commitments as Unitarian Universalists—our unity—and sometimes we accent our independence or our freedom from the larger body—our diversity. As a result we have a deep ambivalence in

We have a deep ambivalence in our attitudes toward congregational polity, even a love-hate relationship.

our attitudes toward congregational polity, even a love-hate relationship. This ambivalence is reflected in several provisions of the fundamental charter of the Association, the UUA Bylaws.

Articles II and III of the Unitarian Universalist Association Bylaws (sections C-2.1 through C-3.3) bear directly or implicitly on the subject of congregational polity. Examining these provisions also points to certain tensions and unresolved questions in the provisions themselves.

"We covenant . . . "

Section C-2.1 [Article 2, Section 1], Principles, begins and ends with the assertion that the UUA is constituted by a "covenant" into which "we, the member congregations" enter. The Cambridge Platform of 1648 reflected the biblical concept of a covenant between God and "the people of God," under "the Lordship of Christ." These ideas were central in the theology of the New England Puritans, from which American Unitarianism derives. Their congregations, a significant number of which became Unitarian in the early nineteenth century, expressed their "bond of unity"—their common faith and purpose—in the form of covenants. These covenants remained in use among these churches long after the ancient Christian creeds had fallen into disuse.

Today, the term "covenant" is often used to explain how a "non-creedal" church can assert its unity of purpose (if not necessarily its unity of belief). To our knowledge, "covenant" had not been used in any official document until the adoption of the UUA Principles statement in 1985, indicating a stronger bond among congregations in the Unitarian Universalist movement than before.

The Principles statement is also covenantal in form. It states seven commitments to shared values and—implicitly, if not explicitly—beliefs; these commitments form the core of the covenant itself. Although the language of these seven statements is open to interpretation, the commitments are stated as moral and spiritual standards that are presumably binding on all member congregations. To this extent, the independence of our congregations is sharply qualified.

In some cases it is unclear whether the seven Principles are addressed to congregations or to individuals. For example, "a free and responsible search for truth and meaning" could be directed to either. This ambiguity is characteristic of contemporary Unitarian Universalism and raises a question: Is our Association congregationally or individually constituted?

Shared Values and Beliefs

Notably, these Principles are stated as moral ideals, reflecting our very cautious approach to theological affirmations, at least in terms of "we-language." One exception may be the seventh Principle, which can be understood as a vision of ultimate reality: "the interdependent web of all existence of which we are a part." The seventh principle has assumed prominence in recent years, probably because it reflects ecological ideals and resonates spiritually with our times. Although there is no uniform or authoritative interpretation of the Principles, the seventh Principle is sometimes given a quasi-creedal aura. We see this when it is used as a statement of shared beliefs and values, or recited in church services, or used to justify resolutions of social issues, or used to ground religious education curricula.

The second part of the Principles statement begins: "The living tradition which we share draws from many sources." Religious as distinct from secular covenants are grounded in spiritual realities that were understood traditionally as divine gifts; for these gifts the people entering the covenant acknowledged gratitude. James Luther Adams has emphasized that an authentic covenant is rooted in love, not law. Rules and regulations are secondary to the originating motive of the covenant. The sources section of the UUA Principles statement fulfills this motivating function by saying, in effect: We are grateful for being heirs to a "living tradition" that has taken these diverse forms. The psychic impact of this understanding is immense. To the extent that consciousness of a cherished common heritage is strong among us, our sense of unity is also strong.

An authentic covenant is rooted in love, not law.

Legitimating Diversity

Presumably, we draw significant meaning from all six sources, whatever our personal beliefs or our congregation's theological stance. However, the sources section also legitimates Unitarian Universalist diversity by implying that the following traditions all contribute to a common living tradition: mystical, prophetic, universal, Jewish/Christian, Humanist, and earth-centered. The legitimation of theological diversity is made explicit: "Grateful for the religious pluralism. . . ." Thus the inclusive principle is also a protective principle, as if to say, "You can't read any one group out of the fold."

The sources section of the Principles acknowledges theological subgroups as distinct from complete individualism (the idea that each of us decides for ourselves what to believe). This seems to be another new sign of our willingness to use "we-language" in theology. In fact, several subgroups with specific theological identities have emerged among us and have gained prominence in recent years, for example, Pagans, Christians, Jews, Buddhists, and Humanists!

This diversity may seem a positive gain (both in terms of our inclusiveness and willingness to make substantive theological or spiritual affirmations). But it also has a cost; because some of the six sources are identified with particular subgroups of Unitarian Universalism itself, the sources remind us of our lack of theological unity.

The sources section also raises the question: What about other subgroups? Whom have we left out or excluded? Indeed, is any group excluded, and if so, on what basis? Are other subgroups subsumed under existing categories (as those primarily concerned with unity argue), or do they require explicit mention (as those primarily concerned with diversity argue)? If so, will we begin to add any number of new subgroups, suggesting further fracturing of Unitarian Universalist unity? Are we a religion with no unifying core, or do we hold that all of these sources are derived from a common spiritual reality—that our diversity represents different refractions of the same light?

An Association or a Movement?

To what extent is it possible for us to affirm and live by a strong sense of community among our autonomous congregations?

Unitarian Universalism, or the Unitarian Universalist movement, is more than the UUA, even though the UUA functions as an umbrella under which the congregations and other institutions and organizations are gathered. The Principles section of the UUA Bylaws directly precedes the Purposes, presumably because principles are more basic than the institutional purposes of the organization; indeed, one of the several Purposes of the UUA is "to implement its principles." There is, then, a curious symmetry in the Principles section: On the one hand, the UUA is an institution wholly constituted by its member congregations, each with its own commitments; on the other hand, the congregations that enter into covenant with each other are bound by a set of common commitments. Each depends on the other—in "the interdependent web of all existence of which we are a part."

These questions hinge on a host of different attitudes and understandings and yield no simple answers. Their deep relevance to congregational polity is to heighten our awareness of the question, To what extent is it possible for us to affirm and live by a strong sense of community among our autonomous congregations?

Other provisions of UUA Bylaws are also pertinent to the theme of congregational polity. Commentary follows.

Briefer comments on other provisions of the UUA Bylaws follow. Although those sections do not attract as much attention as does the Principles section, they are pertinent to the theme of congregational polity.

Why Congregations Need the UUA

Section C-2.2 of the Bylaws, Purposes, states the purposes of the UUA itself. First, "religious, educational and humanitarian purposes" are named. This broad statement allows the Association wide latitude to act in ways that may or may not be relevant to its member congregations; notably, from the perspective of congregational polity, it empowers the UUA to be much more than merely the creature of its constituent groups. Although the UUA is ultimately governed by the congregations, the mechanism of the Board of Trustees enables the Association to own and raise funds (from foundations, individuals, endowments, fees, etc.) independent of its member congregations.

Second, the UUA's "primary purpose" is described, namely "to serve the needs of its member congregations, organize new congregations, extend and strengthen Unitarian Universalist institutions and implement its principles." This statement quickly gathers up a host of functions. The first purpose, serving the needs of existing congregations, ties the UUA directly to its constituent bodies and implies a responsive relationship to their needs.

The second purpose, organizing new congregations, is a function that congregations seldom undertake by themselves, even though they often work with the Association in this task. Congregational polity in its narrow sense does not serve the needs of the Unitarian Universalist movement in the forming of new congregations, which is also a source of tension among existing congregations. For instance, a new congregation may be started in a location that an existing congregation considers its turf. However, the UUA recognizes no exclusive territorial rights.

The third purpose, strengthening other Unitarian Universalist institutions, such as theological schools, international associations, and various other groups, is also something that congregations do not typically do effectively. This function is important to the identification of individuals with the Unitarian Universalist movement beyond the local congregation.

The fourth purpose, "implementing its principles"—presumably an explicit reference to the Principles of the UUA—is another important extra-congregational function. For instance, if asked why we pass General Resolutions at General Assemblies, we might reply, "To implement our principles." Taking this purpose seriously would raise many questions about our practice of congregational polity. For instance, do the governance structure and General Assembly of the UUA truly reflect our commitment to the democratic process? Would a more robust practice of congregational polity serve to renew democratic governance in the UUA, for example, by having delegates who hold leadership positions in their congregations transact significant business of the Association?

Individualism or Common Commitment?

Section C-2.3, Non-discrimination, commits the UUA and its member congregations to both a negative principle of non-discrimination and a positive principle of "full participation" in "the full range of human endeavor." Race, color, sex, disability, affectional or sexual orientation, age, national origin, and religious belief are specifically listed. One of the most hotly contested issues of congregational polity was the addition of this section to the Constitution at the 1963 General Assembly; objections that this provision interfered with the autonomy of the congregations were overcome at a subsequent General Assembly, when this amendment was added. The section speaks of this provision as our "special responsibility," apparently to accent that non-discrimination and social inclusiveness go to the heart of Unitarian Universalist principles.

Section C-2.4, Freedom of Belief, reads: "Nothing herein shall be deemed to infringe upon the individual freedom of belief which is inherent in the Universalist and Unitarian heritages or to conflict with any statement of purposes, covenant, bond of union used by any society unless such is used as a creedal test." This sentence is loaded with strongly stated principles, some of which are in tension (and potentially in conflict) with other constitutional provisions.

Notably, individualism is here enshrined in the idea of "individual freedom of belief"; a wag might say that this is the one dogma of our non-dogmatic faith. The ethos of individualism deeply affects the ways in which we view both our congregations and the UUA; this is probably the major element of Unitarian Universalism today that makes corporate commitment difficult to achieve. Such a radically anti-institutional principle as this "liberty clause" implies that whatever else is said in the Bylaws, the individual member has priority over the whole body.

This statement also implies that congregations—at least in formal affirmations—are independent of the constitutional authority of the UUA; no congregation is required to adopt the UUA Principles even though they have covenanted to "affirm and support" them. One exception to this assertion of congregational autonomy is stipulated, namely, the use of a congregational statement as a creedal test; in other words, the individual is a higher authority than the congregation.

What we see here is a system that involves several mutual limitations placed on the individual, the congregation, and the Association. Although the system seems to be full of inner contradictions, in practice, apparently, it works.

Section 3-1.1, Member Societies, is a formal definition of the UUA: "a voluntary association of autonomous, self-governing local churches and fellowships." This definition briefly and precisely establishes the principle of congregational polity as the primary, defining form of religious community. By implication, the UUA and the Unitarian Universalist movement are secondary, dependent on the congregations, even though other constitutional provisions imply that the UUA is also autonomous, with a life of its own.

Congregational Polity: Rights or Shibboleth?

Section 3-1.2, Congregational Polity, deserves to be cited in its entirety:

> Nothing in these Bylaws shall be construed as infringing upon the congregational polity or internal self-government of member societies, including the exclusive right of each such society to call and ordain its own minister or ministers, and to control its own property and funds. Any action by a member society called for by these Bylaws shall be deemed to have been taken if certified by an authorized officer of the society as having been duly and regularly taken in accordance with its own procedures and the laws which govern it.

The last sentence ensures that the UUA will honor the duly appointed officers of any member society. The first sentence is notable as another liberty clause, treating congregational polity purely as a negative or protective principle, like the colonial New Hampshire motto, "Don't Tread on Me." It says nothing about honoring the positive value of the congregation as a vital center of spiritual, moral, and social life in communities of mutual concern and interpersonal relationships. No wonder that we think of congregational polity as a bastion of independence rather than as an agency of interdependence.

Two important rights are asserted as inherent in congregational polity. One is the right of each congregation "to call and ordain its own ministers" (reiterated in Article XI, Ministry). This right is well established in the UUA. A narrow understanding of congregational polity would imply that only called and settled ministers are truly ministers; then installation would be tantamount to ordination. But in fact, we have never carried the congregational idea this far; rather, we follow the ancient tradition of clerical ordination, in which ordination is recognized by the entire community of congregations as once and for all (an "indelible sacrament" in Catholic theology). As a result, the UUA function of Fellowshipping people considered qualified for ministry in any of our congregations has become more important than ordination. The ordination ceremony has tended to become a mere ceremony. This is one of the most striking ways in which we do not keep with congregational polity. Although a congregation is free to call and ordain its own clergy, only clergy in Fellowship may be ministerial delegates to the General Assembly. Congregations without Fellowshipped clergy therefore have less representation in the Association.

The other right reserved to the congregations is "to control its own property and funds." Indeed, the congregations are normally expected to be wholly self-supporting, although they may sometimes receive subsidies for specific purposes such as paying an extension minister or a low-interest building loan.

A special situation is the disbursal of the property and funds of a congregation that dissolves. The law requires that remaining assets be transferred to another non-profit organization to avoid giving benefits to individuals. The UUA requires that congregations seeking admission have a provision in their bylaws specifying that the UUA will receive any remaining assets on dissolution. However, many congregations joined before this policy was created, and nothing prevents a congregation from changing its bylaws once it is admitted.

Missing: A Positive Vision

What seems missing from the UUA Bylaws is a positive vision of the congregation and the web of interrelationships.

Section 3.3, Admission to Membership, provides that "a church or fellowship may become a member society" when the UUA Board of Trustees accepts its application; it also specifies that the applicant group must state that it "subscribes to the principles of and pledges to support the Association." It is not apparent whether "the principles" referred to are the Principles in Article C-2.1. Nevertheless, this provision represents a strong basis for unity among our "community of autonomous congregations." The requirement of financial support has not been pressed until recently. We view this requirement as salutary; in the past the Association, fearing the loss of member congregations, has been reluctant to require financial support, thus weakening itself in the eyes of its members.

Section C-3.5 sets three minimal standards for certification of "a member society." A church or fellowship must have "(1) conducted regular religious services; (2) held at least one business meeting of its members, elected its own officers and maintained adequate records of membership; and (3) made a financial contribution to the Association." Beyond this there is no requirement that member societies be bound by the policies or decisions of official committees (such as the Board of Review or the Ministerial Fellowship Committee).

The provisions of this section are as far as we have gone in limiting the autonomy of the local congregation; apart from the Principles section, which ring with Unitarian Universalist idealism and commitment, the UUA Bylaws are predominantly a legal document, delimiting the authority of the central body and setting only minimal standards for participation. What seems missing is a positive vision of the congregation and the web of interrelationships, including but not limited to the UUA, on which its vitality and, indeed, its authenticity, depend.

Summary

A review of these constitutional provisions reminds us that the nature and well-being of congregations are never addressed in the fundamental document of the Unitarian Universalist Association. No doubt this is because the Bylaws apply to the UUA and refer to the congregations only in their relation to that institution. The Bylaws do not reflect the idea that constituent congregations of the UUA have corporate ministries, relating them to a continental or universal religious body. Nevertheless, especially in the Principles section, the Bylaws make assertions about Unitarian Universalism as a moral and spiritual commitment of individual persons and of the Association's constituent congregations. We would have a stronger sense of *the community of autonomous congregations* if we more fully stated the purposes for which the congregations exist.

Recommendation

Unitarian Universalist leaders should generate a proposed amendment to the UUA Bylaws that describes the constituent members of the UUA—the congregations—in a way that gives positive meaning to the principle of congregational polity. Such an amendment would say that congregational polity is not only a principle to protect local autonomy; it also affirms the interdependence of the congregations as essential to their spiritual vitality and authenticity.

SECTION FIVE

The Spiritual and Cultural Ethos of Unitarian Universalism

The collective personality of any group reflects both conscious and unconscious patterns that express the group's way of being in the world and its relationship with its members. This section explores how our collective identity—our ethos—and our often unconscious ideas, feelings, and cultural expressions—our mythos—underpin our understanding of congregational polity and hinder our efforts to create a community of autonomous congregations.

If Unitarian Universalists proudly display the axiom "Question Authority," it is because we are genuinely uncomfortable with power. If we acknowledge the legitimacy of power in any venue, we often view it as a negative force or at least suspiciously. This is a core dynamic of our identity as Unitarian Universalists. In this context, how we work together as a voluntary religious movement becomes a very complex question because to quote the Commission on Appraisal's 1983 report, "voluntary consensus is put on a collision course with the needs of the larger organizational structure to exercise democratically achieved forms of power."[1]

How we govern ourselves may represent the most obvious dimension of congregational polity, but if we are to understand polity more fully, we must place it in the context of other aspects of our collective identity—who we are as Unitarian Universalists. Although the principles of democracy and congregational autonomy are central to our identity, there are other key elements. Our group identity—how we see ourselves—affects many key aspects of our congregational life and culture: how we think about mission; how we present ourselves to the world; how we worship and celebrate; how we understand our philosophical, ethical, moral, and

Sometimes our attitudes run counter to the principles we say that we hold dear.

theological foundations; the issues that express our interests and highest values; our perceptions of and relationships with others, especially those we perceive as unlike ourselves.

Our Ethos: Who We Are as Unitarian Universalists

Ethos can be understood as our collective identity and personality: how we as Unitarian Universalists present ourselves to each other and the world.

Demographic data is one measure of our ethos. Market research conducted in 1987 from which the UUA collected both demographic and psychographic (or lifestyle) data, as well as the 1990 National Survey of Religious Identification (NSRI), are instructive in understanding our dominant cultural ethos and identity. The NSRI survey[2] ranks Unitarian Universalists highest among 30 religious movements in aggregate social status on "Protestant ethic variables," which include level of education, household income, extent of home ownership, and patterns of employment. (Both these surveys were limited to the United States.) The following profile of Unitarian Universalists emerges from the NSRI survey:

- Unitarian Universalists are the most highly educated (49.5 percent are college educated and many have earned advanced degrees)
- Unitarian Universalists enjoy the second-highest median household income ($34,800 per annum)
- Nearly three out of four Unitarian Universalists own their homes (73.2 percent, and tenth in rank order)
- More than half hold full-time jobs (52.8 percent, and eleventh in rank order).

A 1987 Association-commissioned demographic and psychographic survey[3] amplifies this profile, reporting that the typical Unitarian Universalist is

- 52 years old (down from 55 in a 1987 survey)
- more likely to be a woman than a man
- of European-American heritage
- nature-oriented and living in a suburban community
- politically active and environmentally conscious.

Significantly, when this survey was presented to the Association, it was pointed out that this profile was an exact match with the customers on the catalog mailing list of L.L. Bean. In 1992, *World* magazine conducted a reader profile (updating the 1987 demographic survey) that indicated no significant changes in the UU profile.[4]

Unitarian Universalists as Liberal Religionists

Recent studies of congregational life in the United States expand the picture of who we are as liberal religionists. In his book, *U.S. Lifestyles and Mainline Churches,* for example, church historian Tex Sample defines three groups as the *cultural left, cultural center*, and *cultural right*. While these categories do not necessarily correspond to political labels, the group that Sample defines as the cultural left is quite consistent with the demographic and psychographic profiles of Unitarian Universalists described above. According to Sample, members of the cultural left:

- are strongly inner directed
- have a self-fulfillment orientation
- tend to be nonconformists
- have little loyalty to authority or institutions (little respect for "God, country, or apple pie")
- are politically liberal
- are mostly affluent
- are deeply concerned about social issues, especially peace, the environment, and consumer issues
- are nature centered, often believing strongly that "nature has its own wisdom"
- tend to be experimental, particularly in terms of theology
- are often not members of religious institutions
- tend to seek the mystical
- are often attracted to Eastern religions.

The UUA's market research suggests that Unitarian Universalists are largely suburbanites. In a study conducted in May 1982, Roof and McKinney[5] found that 44 percent of Unitarian Universalists live in suburbs, but that nearly one-third (31 percent) live in large cities. This report does not take into account that many of our congregations are located in small cities and towns. In contrast, the highest percentage of Canadian Unitarians live in big cities and suburbs. Historically, the greatest concentration of Unitarian Universalists in the United States is in the Northeast (33 percent), but a growing percentage now resides in the Midwest.

Given our history, as well as the high concentration of congregations in New England, it is not surprising that Unitarian Universalism has been called "the Boston religion," which carries the flavor and personality of the European-American upper classes. This characterization is still very much at the heart of Unitarian Universalist identity, as is a tendency toward the logical and the rational, which is not surprising given the history of the Free Church movement so firmly rooted in the Enlightenment era.[6]

The "Religion of the Successful"

The religion of the successful turns out to be a sham spirituality for it tends to reduce itself to personal kindliness and philanthropy costing little.

What emerges from this data is a picture of the "paramount value pattern"[7] of our religious movement. These statistical profiles also support the claim that Unitarian Universalism has a "long history of high status in this society."[8] James Luther Adams addresses the theological implications of this status in what he calls "the religion of the successful":

> We [in the United States] live in neighborhoods segregated from other neighborhoods in terms of education, occupation, and income; also separated by class and pigmentation, that is, by race. The segregation of sexism cuts across all of these boundaries. In all too great a measure, the churches are a function and indeed a protection of these segregations.
>
> In this situation, we of the middle class are tempted, indeed almost fated, to adopt the religion of the successful. This religion of the successful amounts to a systematic concealment of and separation from reality—a hiding of the plight of those who in one sense or another live across the tracks. In the end, this concealment comes from a failure to identify correctly and to enter into combat with what St. Paul called "the principalities and powers of evil." The religion of the successful turns out then to be a sham spirituality, a cultivated blindness, for it tends to reduce itself to personal kindliness and philanthropy costing little. Thus it betrays the world with a kiss.[9]

H. Richard Niebuhr suggests that these characteristics are not specific to Unitarian Universalism, but are representative of middle-class denominations:

> . . . the psychology of the [United States] middle class contains certain constant features which are reflected in its religious organizations and doctrines. Among these, the most important are the high development of individual self-consciousness and the prevalence of an activist attitude toward life.[10]

Niebuhr views class, race, national origin, and regionalism as social factors that are more important than theology in shaping the religious landscape in the United States, however much we might prefer this conclusion to be inaccurate.

Coming to Terms With Our Mythos

In addition to our ethos, our *mythos*—the often unconscious ideas, feelings, and cultural expressions that many Unitarian Universalists in the United States hold—may also be important to understanding our collective identity.

Some people in our faith are concerned that there are psychosocial dimensions of the culture of Unitarian Universalism that are not easily characterized. One such quality is what some people call "anal retentiveness"—the tendency toward orderliness (to the point of perfectionism), rigidity, stinginess, and obstinacy. Others have pointed out that a part of our collective personality is a tendency to be haughty, self-righteous, controlling and to express moral superiority. Two traits—self-righteousness and individualism—require further exploration.

Self-Righteousness

It is ironic that although freedom and tolerance are central pillars of our faith, we can be somewhat intolerant, owing at least in part to our tendency toward self-righteousness. The Reverend Barbara Merritt describes this proclivity:

> We can put up all kinds of signs around our church buildings, declaring our enlightenment, our openness and our glorious political consensus. With such advertisements we communicate two very important messages to visitors. First, those of us who attend this church are politically correct and publicly virtuous. Second, if you disagree with any of our pronouncements, causes or solutions, your opinion will not be heard, valued or taken seriously.[11]

Sometimes our attitudes run counter to the principles we say that we hold dear. On the one hand, we say that we affirm "the inherent worth and dignity of every person," value civil liberties, and promote tolerance and freedom of speech. On the other hand, our self-righteous attitudes are anything but tolerant and open to diverse viewpoints. Merritt traces this tendency toward moral superiority to the early history of the Unitarian movement. As an illustration, she cites T. S. Eliot's understanding of his Unitarian relatives:

> To be a Unitarian, "was to be noble, upright, and superior to all other human beings . . . Unitarians believed that they were already enlightened, the enlightenment for them was an intellectual achievement. . . . Unitarians were put on earth to better the lot of humanity, to be a good and inspiring example. . . . Unitarians were expected to be dutiful, be-

nevolent, cheerful, self-restrained and unemotional. . . . They attended church to set a good example to others."[12]

Psychologist Richard Kevin, a member of the Unitarian Universalist Fellowship in Raleigh, North Carolina, explains the same tendency:

> UUs in one-church towns are somewhat like isolated aboriginal societies who have no word for human being in their language other than the word for themselves. Such groups find the discovery of human beings who are not of their tribe profoundly disturbing.[13]

If self-righteousness is one area where a need for growth is indicated, so too are communication and intolerance. One of our ministers who preferred to remain anonymous, agreed with Richard Kevin, but went further:

> One of the results [of our difficulty in understanding others as human] is that we not only feel this way, but that we feel we are entitled to be the definers of reality and of "the right way" to be in the world. A corollary is that only a select few are sufficiently evolved to be among us.

These characteristics are among the paradoxes of our cultural ethos and group identity as Unitarian Universalists that often lead us into conflict.

Individualism

Strident individualism is an impediment to building alliances and allegiance among our congregations, the Association, and the larger community.

Individualism has been a core value in the United States since its inception and has grown stronger in the larger culture, including religious institutions and Unitarian Universalism. (As discussed further on, in Canada, individualism does not seem to be a primary value.) Within Unitarian Universalism, church historian Conrad Wright credits both Thomas Jefferson and Ralph Waldo Emerson as exemplars of "the extreme individualism that has been a hallmark of liberal religion," and as "privatized" so that their views "can yield no rationale for religious fellowship in general or the Church in particular."[14]

In a 1993 sermon on individualism, the Reverend John Papandrew (a Unitarian Universalist minister for more than 40 years) suggests that as an ethic, individualism ultimately fails us, with worrisome theological implications: "There is a vast underworld of people who have lived with the fantasy of the Lone Ranger and found it to be Hell. For Hell is the absence of relationship—the ultimate disconnection."[15]

Most Unitarian Universalist congregations hold an allegiance primarily to themselves, with only a secondary allegiance to the Association, districts, and related Unitarian Universalist organs. In spite of strong social action/social justice programs in many congregations, an allegiance to the larger community is often missing.

What causes this distancing and insularity? A partial answer may lie in the high value placed on rugged individualism, or in what Dieter Hessel called "strident individualism." Psychiatrist M. Scott Peck discusses this phenomenon from a theological perspective:

> The problem—indeed the total failure—of the "ethic" of rugged individualism is that it . . . incorporates only one half of our humanity. It recognizes that we are called to individuation, power, and wholeness. But it denies entirely the other part of the human story; that we can never fully get there and that we are, of necessity, in our uniqueness, weak and imperfect creatures who need each other. . . . It also relentlessly isolates us from each other. And it makes genuine community impossible.[16]

While Peck's statement does not specifically discuss Unitarian Universalism, his analysis suggests that strident individualism is an impediment to building alliances and allegiance among our congregations, the Association, and the larger community. An additional consequence may be the loss of relational values that we take for granted: love, compassion, loyalty, service, justice—which some people understand as the goal of building *a beloved community*.

A Distinctive Canadian Ethos

Canadian Unitarian Universalists generally value the ethic of community more highly than that of individualism. The ethos of Canadian Unitarian Universalists—who live in the shadow of the United States, with a fraction of its population and an even smaller percentage of the UU family—has developed under the influence of and in reaction to Unitarian Universalists in the United States. Canadians still debate whether the ethos of our religious movement is that of Unitarians or Unitarian Universalists.

Whereas Unitarian thought moved into and across Canada both from the United States and from Europe (primarily England and Iceland), Universalist thought penetrated mainly into Ontario and Nova Scotia. By the time the two movements merged in Canada (a few months before the US merger), there was only a handful of Universalist congregations.

Much of the Canadian ethos has developed in relation to the "elephant next door," as the United States is often called. Those who live within the shadow of a dominant group with a dominant ideology often find themselves defined and self-defining in relation to the larger, ever-present "other."

Unlike its neighbor to the south, the Canadian cry is not for independence and freedom as the utmost values, but for peace, order, and good government.

With the explosion of electronic information processing, Canadians have more access to United States culture than to Canadian. For example, although there are only two national television networks in Canada (CBC and CTV), most cable systems carry at least the major three US national networks in addition to a host of cable-only stations.

Despite this strong cultural presence, however, a prominent aspect of the Canadian Unitarian ethos is the insistence that it is *not* American. This seeming paradox may lie in the origins of each nation: Whereas the United States was founded as a national entity through armed insurrection, Canada was founded through legislation passed by the British Parliament in 1867. Unlike its neighbor to the south, the Canadian cry is not for independence and freedom as the utmost values, but for peace, order, and good government. Canadians tend to believe that the government is responsible for providing the necessities of life: programs and policies that guarantee access to basic food, housing, education, unemployment insurance, and health care, for which there is a collective responsibility to pay through higher tax rates. Despite a shift within the last five to ten years toward individual responsibility for these social needs, Canadians still believe that government should retain overall responsibility for the well-being of its people.

This understanding helps to explain the difference in beliefs about the basic unit of society. In the United States, the unit is the individual and the basic responsibility of government is to ensure the individual's right to freedom; in Canada the basic unit is the collective, and the government's responsibility is to provide for its citizens. This collective is variously defined as national, ethnic (First Peoples, Francophones, Icelandics, Ukrainians, etc.), provincial, regional, or local.

Within Canadian congregational life, the basic unit is most often the congregation or occasionally a subgroup within the congregation, but not individual members. A wider identification is also made with the cluster or region (where there are enough congregations to have a cluster); with the district (this is particularly true for the Western Canada District, the only entirely Canadian district); and with the Canadian Unitarian Council (CUC). Links outside national boundaries are more likely to be formed with the International Council of Unitarians and Universalists (ICUU) or with the International Association for Religious Freedom (IARF) rather than with the UUA.

Tensions Between Canada and the United States

Frequently Canadian Unitarians point out that their "American cousins" do not understand the particularities of Canada and the religious movement north of the border. For example, at General Assemblies, the Actions of Social Witness and Statements of Immediate Witness tend to deal only with issues in the United States, or assume that Canadian and United States issues are identical; this does injustice to Canada's uniqueness. Another source of tension lies in the methods suggested for annual canvass programs, which are not adapted to the sensitivity of Canadians in talking about money. At the same time, the rate of fair-share congregations is higher in Canada than in the United States—despite the fact that fair-share contributions through the Canadian Unitarian Council and district dues are higher for most Canadian congregations than for their US counterparts.

Tension often arises when Canadian congregations search for professional leadership. Clergy candidates from the United States may not fully understand that Canada is a different country, with a different history and culture. Congregations may invest time and money before the candidates realize the importance of their own national roots and withdraw from consideration. At times like these, Canadian congregations realize the size of the American elephant.

An anti-American, anti-UUA attitude also affects US clergy serving in Canada. Sometimes statements and observations made by US clergy are dismissed as being "American," or from a US perspective that is out of touch with Canadian values or ethos. The same statements are more likely to be accepted when made by Canadian clergy.

The prevailing notion of peace, order, and good government does not leave much room for acknowledging conflict within congregational life. In contrast to those from the United States, Canadians are often reticent about dealing with conflict openly, which can frustrate many US clergy and expatriate members of Canadian congregations.

Building a Community of Autonomous Congregations

The Canadian ethos and identity have important ramifications for the issue of congregational polity in congregations throughout North America. Although one central recommendation of this report—the building of a *community* of autonomous congregations—may be more readily accepted within the Canadian Unitarian movement, Canadians may be resistant to any understanding of polity that does not take into account the differing reality of Unitarianism in Canada.

Only to the extent that we remember and honor the very real and closely held differences that exist between the two nations will we be able to create a single community of autonomous congregations. However, by looking carefully at the success of the Canadian Unitarian Council—with its reliance on collectivity rather than individualism—we may create a better framework for becoming a community of autonomous congregations.

Summary

Who we are as Unitarian Universalists and as religious liberals is not coincidental to how we interpret congregational polity and rely on it to justify our understandings or positions.

Our demographic characteristics both strengthen and stifle our progress. The fact that (generally speaking) we are a highly educated group of people in positions of influence serves us well. Yet these same characteristics sometimes lead to blind spots about those whose demographic characteristics are inconsistent with our own, and sometimes to a false sense of moral superiority as well. Similarly, our outlook on power is both a strength and a limitation. We have a healthy disrespect for the legitimacy of power, so perhaps it is not surprising that power conflicts are often contentious. Similarly, values such as individualism are consistent with the value of freedom. At the same time, individualism is supported at the expense of building community.

"Strident individualism" is a fundamental value in the United States, in contrast to the more collective values of Canadians—a factor that demands our attention if we are to move toward building a stronger community of autonomous congregations. Exploring some of the factors that characterize the cultural ethos and identity of Unitarian Universalism provides a basis for considering in Part 2 of this report the pressure points of congregational polity—those areas of conflict that prevent us from more fully entering and building right relationships.

Recommendation

To understand more fully those areas in which our practice of congregational polity may affect our religious community both positively and negatively, congregations should engage in a process of study and reflection on how our collective identity—our ethos—and our unconscious values and beliefs—our mythos—may strengthen or limit our understanding of what it means to be a pluralistic religious movement.

Sources

Conversations with Eleanor Maticka-Tyndale, sociologist, University of Windsor; Sanford Tyndale; Brian Kiely, minister of South Fraser Unitarian Congregation, Surrey, British Columbia; Diane Miller, director, Department of Ministry; Tracey Robinson-Harris, deputy director, Department for Congregational, District and Extension Services; Lisa Presley, former interim minister, Unitarian Church of Calgary, Alberta; and William Sinkford, director, Department for Congregational, District and Extension Services.

Notes

1. Unitarian Universalist Association, *EmPowerment: One Denomination's Quest for Racial Justice 1967-1982*, Report of the Unitarian Universalist Commission on Appraisal to the General Assembly, June 1983 (Boston: Unitarian Universalist Association, 1984).
2. Barry A. Kosmin and Seymour P. Lachman, *One Nation Under God* (New York: Harmony Books, 1993), p. 257.
3. Peter Heiurichs, "Boom or Bust? What Market Research Tells Us About the Future of Unitarian Universalism," report of survey results presented to the UUA, September 26, 1987.
4. *World* Reader Profile Survey. Readex. (Boston: Unitarian Universalist Association, 1992 and 1996).
5. Wade Clark Roof and William McKinney, *American Mainline Religion* (New Brunswick, New Jersey: Rutgers University Press, 1987).
6. See essays by James Luther Adams, "Natural Religion and the 'Myth' of the Eighteenth Century," in *The Prophethood of All Believers*, ed. by George K. Beach (Boston: Beacon Press, 1986), and "Conversations at Collegium" and "The Liberal Christian Holds Up the Mirror," in *An Examined Faith*, ed. by George K. Beach (Boston: Beacon Press, 1991).
7. John Madge, *Origins of Scientific Sociology* (New York: Free Press, 1962), p. 241.
8. Barry A. Kosmin and Seymour P. Lachman, *One Nation Under God*.
9. James Luther Adams, "Hidden Evils and Hidden Resources," *The Prophethood of All Believers*, p. 83.
10. H. Richard Niebuhr, *The Social Sources of Denominationalism* (New York: New American Library, 1929), pp. 80-81.
11. Barbara Merrit, "In Opposition to the Resolution: A Subtle Tyranny," *Unitarian Universalist Voice*, Summer 1995, Vol. 1, No. 2, pp. 4-5.
12. *Ibid.*
13. Quoted by Warren Ross, "Diversity Without Division: Theological Difference in Our Congregations and How To Make It Work For You," *World*, November/December 1996, Vol. x, No. 6, p. 36.
14. David Robinson, *The Unitarians and the Universalists* (Westport, CT: Greenwood Press, 1985), p. 156.
15. John Papandrew, "Individualism: It Ain't Necessarily So," sermon, November 14, 1993, All Souls Church, Washington, DC.
16. M. Scott Peck, *The Different Drum: Community Making and Peace* (New York: Simon and Schuster, 1987), p. 56.

PART TWO

Pressure Points: Issues and Concerns Related to Congregational Polity

Within our congregations and in the associations that link congregations and individual Unitarian Universalists, we experience many pressures for change—change in our lay and professional leadership, our ways of addressing social-ethical concerns, how we seek numerical and financial growth, or how we connect among our congregations. These pressures commonly generate tensions; sometimes they are met by counterpressures, because the changes are perceived as unwelcome or even destructive of cherished values. In this report we use the term "pressure points" to characterize the places in our institutional life where tensions and conflicts arise.

Part 2 examines tensions that have developed between the idea of congregational polity and important institutional needs, goals, and practices. We believe that an inadequate understanding or development of polity is often at the root of these unresolved institutional concerns and problems. Part 2 analyzes seven pressure points in our associational life and makes specific recommendations for action by various denominational bodies. These pressure points, which correspond to the seven sections of Part 2, include:

1. the need to value the process of governance within congregational life as much as we value individualism;
2. the need to strengthen cooperative relationships among our congregations at all levels for our mutual benefit;
3. the need for increased communications among congregations through both print and new electronic media;
4. the need to reshape our understandings of lay and professional ministries, both to resolve current tensions and to meet new needs for religious leadership;

5. the need to develop new forms of religious community and cooperation to be more fully engaged in social justice concerns;
6. the need to recognize that in spite of our professed desire for greater diversity many groups feel marginalized and excluded;
7. the need to build structures that will facilitate the engagement of congregations with liberal religious bodies internationally.

We ask such questions as these: Does congregational polity, as Unitarian Universalists understand and practice it, enable them to deal effectively with these pressure points, or does it frustrate such attempts? To what extent is a congregation purely autonomous, and to what extent is it accountable to the larger community of churches and fellowships? Will greater accountability weaken congregations as self-responsible religious communities, or will it strengthen them?

SECTION SIX

Congregational Governance

One important way that we express our congregational polity is in the governance of our congregations. Governance is spelled out in the fifth Principle, which calls for "the use of the democratic process within our congregations." Just as Unitarian Universalists emphasize—in our theology and history—the independence of each congregation rather than our interdependence through the UUA, we emphasize the independence of each person more than our interdependence as members of a congregation. The tensions between the independent congregations and the Association are analogous to the tensions between the individual and the church community. This section considers how our notions of polity affect the ways we govern our congregations. It offers suggestions for improvement in the areas of decision making; board, ministerial, and congregational relationships; freedom of the pulpit; membership; mutual accountability; money; and stewardship.

Congregational polity is concerned not only with interrelationships among congregations, but also with the governance process of each congregation. Under congregational polity each congregation is self-governing, choosing its own leadership, handling its own finances, and choosing its own delegates to the General Assembly (UUA Bylaws, Sections C-3.2, C-11.1, 4.8). However, this independence does not imply that we must reinvent our governance process in each congregation. Yet we provide few guidelines for congregations to follow.

Our polity is very much responsible for our loose association, which prevents us from prescribing structures and practices for congregations. It

Because the UUA is so often accused of dictating to congregations, the Association, districts, and other congregations are reluctant to suggest congregational practices.

enables organic practices and organizations to rise and survive, which is sometimes a strength, but often does not serve us well. Perhaps because the UUA is so often accused of dictating to congregations, the Association, the districts, and other congregations are reluctant to suggest congregational practices.

The *Congregational Handbook*[1] makes many recommendations for congregational processes. One section addresses Congregational Meetings (p. 89), and an extensive section on bylaws deals with issues such as the power of the board, decision-making processes for the congregation, and elections (p. 33-34). Although the *Handbook* contains much useful information, more could be said on many subjects. For example, the *Handbook* does not mention congregation responsibilities for ordination (discussed in Section 9, "Religious Leadership," in this report), nor does it recommend how delegates to the General Assembly and district meetings are to be selected and instructed. The material that follows touches briefly on several areas that are not fully addressed in the *Handbook*.

Decision Making Within the Congregation

How we relate to each other as individuals within a congregation mirrors the interrelations among congregations, entailing the same issue: balancing independence with interdependence. Difficult decisions such as actions for social justice or a new location for the congregation spark this issue most clearly.

Too often members of congregations believe that the only model for democratic process is for everyone to gather in one place and make all decisions by consensus.

Too often members of congregations believe that the only model for democratic process is for everyone to gather in one place and make all decisions by consensus. Although consensus may be appropriate for a small fellowship, it restricts both the size and development of the congregation. Rabbi and psychotherapist Edwin Friedman states the case: "[Consensus] tends to value peace over progress and personal relationships over ideas. . . . Emphasis on consensus gives strength to the extremists."[2]

The Reverend Brent Smith makes a similar point: "We are not in the tradition of consensus as the chief means of decision making, regardless of its current faddishness amongst us. It is not democratic. It doesn't allow each person to exercise their right to act upon the truth as they see it; that is, to vote. It requires conformity of every person to one decision and one path, and subverts the subtle discernment represented in differing individual viewpoints."[3]

Many congregations use a super-majority to approximate consensus. Their bylaws require a two-thirds or three-quarters vote to call a minister, take a stand on a social justice issue, or sell land. Although it is not democratic in the sense of majoritarian, the difficulty of achieving a super-majority assures that the issue is carefully considered and that most members of the congregation are in agreement. This agreement is particularly important when a congregation takes a stand on a social issue.

Democracy must allow everyone to participate in decisions affecting the group. However, participation might mean delegating a decision to a representative or talking with others before making a significant decision. The important point is for members to be involved in the process. For example, although voting by absentee ballot permits broader participation, it does not encourage members to interact in considering the issue. Its use should be permitted only when members have had adequate opportunity for discussion and debate before voting.

The Reverend Tom Chulak says:

> Without some hierarchy it is my experience that groups become stagnant, orthodox, and rigid. They become oppressive. Why? Because what happens in human community when you do not delegate authority to certain roles and Boards is those who have the greatest need for control and power will move into the center and there will be no way to move these persons out and eventually the group will die. Those groups which do not pay attention to structure—to roles and relationships and the need to have leadership—become the most anti-Unitarian Universalist.[4]

Relationship Between the Board and the Congregation

While our Principles commit us to "the use of the democratic process within our congregations," we are generally unclear about the specifics. For example, which decisions can be made by the board of trustees and when is a vote of the congregation required? What is the specific role of the minister?

Bylaws cannot spell out every decision that must be made by the entire congregation. The appropriate process depends on the size of the congregation. A large congregation must be a representative democracy where most decisions are made by the board; a medium-sized congregation may have more decisions made by the congregation, but many by the board; a small congregation may operate by group consensus. However, as congregations grow they tend to try to function with a decision process suitable to their former size.

We recommend that the bylaws of medium-sized and larger congregations reserve to the full congregation only critical decisions such as the calling of ministers, the approval of the annual budget, and the purchase or sale of land and buildings. A board that is in touch with its membership will bring other decisions to the full congregation when appropriate. For example, approval for a capital campaign may not be required by the bylaws, but would certainly need congregational agreement.

As congregations grow, they tend to try to function with a decision process suitable to their former size.

Again quoting the Reverend Chulak: "I am also a believer that in congregations, we must have a balance of power among staff, Board of Trustees, and the larger congregation. Authority must be distributed.... Balance of authority and power is central to our fulfillment. Within this balance—roles and relationships must be clearly defined."[5]

Relations Between the Board and the Minister

Because the minister is called by the congregation and the board is elected by the congregation, congregations have dual leadership. Congregations that directly elect their officers create a third center of leadership. A board that selects its leadership from among its members avoids a three-way split and creates a more unified board. Whichever method a congregation uses to select its lay leadership, the minister and the lay leaders need to have clearly defined relationships with the congregation, and they must each understand their responsibilities for the congregation's mission.

Ministers have different styles of participating in the governance of a congregation. Some join their churches as members and thus have a vote, although some decide not to use it. (By law in Maryland, clergy must be voting members of their congregation's board.) Some ministers see their role as primarily pastoral, supporting the lay leadership, while others see themselves as consultants, providing experienced advice and suggestions. Still others see themselves as strong leaders, making recommendations to the board and the congregation. An appropriate balance—making the best use of the capabilities of the minister and the congregation—should not be assumed to occur automatically, but be the result of careful consideration, negotiation, and testing.

Ministers often express frustration in getting congregations to make full use of the minister's experience and expertise. Although there is no simple solution to this problem, one suggestion is to have a Committee on Ministry (discussed in "Mutual Accountability" further on in this section). In addition, the expectations of the minister and congregation should be clearly spelled out in the minister's letter of agreement.

Other issues arise from the increasing number of congregations with multiple ministers. Are all ministers supervised by the senior minister? Can there be effective co-ministers who are not married or partnered? The First Unitarian Church in San Francisco has the first co-ministers who applied and were called as unpartnered individuals. Will this be a model for the twenty-first century? The crucial issue, however, is not the form of ministry, but the clarity of the ministers and the congregation about their respective lines of authority.

Freedom of the Pulpit

Freedom of the pulpit traces its roots to the prophets of the Hebrew Bible. *The Congregational Handbook* suggests this bylaw language (p.39): "The minister(s) shall have freedom of the pulpit as well as freedom to express his or her opinion outside the pulpit." This is assumed to mean that while members may express their disagreements, the minister cannot be censured for his or her statements. Although many of our congregations have bylaws that guarantee "freedom of the pulpit," this concept is rarely defined or discussed. The Reverend Thomas Starr King stated his views in a sermon on October 26, 1856:

Our Principles call on us to respect a diversity of opinion, and the freedom of the pulpit should be a part of our cherished tradition.

> Brethren, it isn't a question of what you want to hear, or don't want to hear; it is simply a question of what, with my vision of spiritual laws and human responsibility, *I ought to do*. I have told you how the question looks from my side; and I tell you further, just as honestly, that if you do not like the danger, so long as I shall hold such views, of hearing your public as well as your private responsibilities set thus in the light of them, you have only to say so, in a parish meeting, and the matter will be ended. Even if a large minority will say so, I will give you at once the opportunity of finding a man whose views of duty are different, and whose preaching will be more safe. Let us understand each other on this point, once for all. You certainly have the *right*, as well as the *power*, to choose what type of preaching this pulpit shall represent; so long as I stay in it, it will represent no other type than that I have just described—not because I ever intend to "preach politics," but because I feel I must preach devotion of humanity as the highest outward form of the gospel and the obligation of doing the most good that possibly can be done by all of a man's influence, by his ballot as well as by his money and his words. (emphasis in the original)

This issue is still alive today. For example, is the freedom of the pulpit for anyone speaking from the pulpit, lay or clergy? What is an appropriate response from members of the congregation when something is said that offends them? We recommend that all congregations adhere to a standard of free expression without censure. If most congregants—or even individual members—disagree with something that is said, they should also have the right of dissent. Members can be permitted to address the gathered community without disrupting the worship if limits are set on the time and the place. Such a practice would further democratic expression.

A related issue is the question of who speaks to the public for the congregation? As a religious community, we need to speak out on issues of public policy. However, all members do not necessarily agree on specific stands. The UUA has a well-defined process for the General Assembly to take stands for the UUA. Our congregations rarely have policies that are as clear.

We suggest that congregations consider authorizing the following groups as spokespersons, both to clarify who can speak and to honor possible dissidents:

- The minister(s) of the congregation, indicating his or her title.
- The board of trustees, by majority vote, indicating that they speak as the board, unanimously if that is the case.
- The Social Justice Committee, indicating that it speaks as a committee of the church.
- The members of the congregation, indicating the number of congregants voting in favor or signing the document in question. (See Section 10, "Social Justice," for more information.)

Members of congregations often criticize their ministers for things they have said. In some cases congregations have fired their ministers, notwithstanding the bylaw provision. However, our Principles call on us to respect a diversity of opinion and the freedom of the pulpit should be a part of our cherished tradition.

Membership

The UUA Bylaws state that each member congregation sets its own standards for membership. Although there is no need to change this basic power of congregations within our polity, the result has been a wide variety of procedures and qualifications for membership.

The simplest process is for new members simply to sign a book or other document stating their sympathy with the purposes of the congregation. Some congregations require a pledge of record in a minimum or any amount. Some congregations require an interview with the minister; others require acceptance by the board. Some congregations have age restrictions; others have classes of membership, such as youth. Many congregations have an inactive membership status; the congregation does not count the person but does not sever the relationship. When a person has not contributed or participated for a period of time, the board usually notifies the member of transfer to inactive status. It would be useful to have some survey information about congregations' practices and their effectiveness.

The Congregational Handbook discusses minimum contribution, age, and a waiting period for voting (pp. 35-36). The waiting period is particularly important when membership is open without board approval. For example, if an organized group were to try to join the church to control its assets, a period of 30 to 60 days would enable the church to organize to block the action.

Mutual Accountability

Governance of a congregation is spelled out most clearly in its bylaws. However, custom and practice govern much of the day-to-day operation. Ministry is the task of the whole church—the governing board, minister(s), staff, and membership. How this group works together to further the goals of the church is critical to its success. Understanding that these relationships are based on mutual accountability can help correct the anti-clericism that sometimes occurs in our congregations. While not necessarily spelled out in formal agreements (except, for example, in the minister's letter of agreement), the concept of sharing the ministry of the church is a part of the congregation's polity.

One of the most effective ways to further the mutual accountability of lay leadership, professional leadership, and general membership is through a Committee on Ministry. Although the *Handbook* discusses a Committee on Ministry, its description more closely matches what is generally called a Ministerial Relations Committee.

The Reverend Robert Latham suggests that the Committee on Ministry oversee the entire ministry of the congregation, not just that of the clergy. The Reverend Latham says such a committee has four major areas of responsibility:

1. *Assessment*: responsibility for working out a plan to periodically assess the effectiveness of every facet of congregational ministry.

2. *Communication*: facilitates the flow of communication regarding effective ministry. It promotes dialogue between groups representing various aspects of the congregation's ministry. It seeks a commonality of goals and a webbing of approaches. It engenders trust and mutual respect. It is in consultation with the Board, committees and agents of the congregation's ministry. It makes recommendations whenever and wherever it deems needful in upgrading this ministry. Its approach is always positive rather than negative—always focusing on potential rather than problem.

3. *Education*: since its assessments and recommendations are geared to the congregation's Mission-Covenant, it seeks every opportunity to promote awareness regarding this purpose.

Since the General Assembly has primary responsibility for policy determination for the Association, the General Assembly would be more accountable to the congregations if delegates were elected with care and the cost of attending subsidized if needed.

4. *Consultation*: it is in consultation with the professional ministers as regards effective performance and relationships. It makes recommendations as to salary, benefit and expense packages to the Finance Committee and the Board of Trustees.[6]

Latham adds: "The standard by which all facets of ministry are evaluated is the congregation's statement of Mission-Covenant. Since ministry is everything the congregation does to fulfill its mission, there is no other appropriate standard. To the extent that this Mission-Covenant statement is demanding of responsibility, so is it of accountability."[7]

A Committee on Ministry can do much to foster mutual accountability among clergy, lay leadership, and membership for the advancement of the Mission-Covenant adopted by the congregation. The committee clarifies that the mission is the responsibility of the entire congregation, not just its ordained clergy.

We recommend that the UUA make available to congregations a variety of assessment instruments and procedures for evaluating the ministry of the congregation and clergy, in addition to those already in *The Congregational Handbook*.

There are other ways in which the democratic polity of congregations can enhance mutual accountability. For instance, in most congregations the delegates to the General Assembly are self-selected, based on their interest and financial ability to pay the cost of attending. Since the General Assembly has primary responsibility for policy determination for the Association, the General Assembly would be more accountable to the congregations if delegates were elected with care and the cost of attending subsidized if needed.

One of the most difficult situations a congregation faces is when a member conducts himself or herself in a manner that is severely destructive to the church community. Many, if not most, UU churches have no established procedure for removing such a person from a committee or membership. We recommend that congregations provide in their bylaws a process for terminating membership when a person's actions are contrary to the congregation's purpose and program. This might be done by a supermajority of the board of trustees, with appeal rights of the full congregation to assure due process. Termination could also include a process for reconciliation and readmission.

Personnel

Another difficult area of congregational governance is personnel administration—the hiring, evaluation, supervision, and dismissal of non-clergy staff. Some congregations designate the minister as chief executive officer who oversees the staff. Other congregations delegate this responsibility to the board of trustees or jointly to the board and minister. What is important is that the responsibility for personnel be clear and understood by all. Personnel should be evaluated regularly and in writing; conditions of employment should also be in writing.

Money and Giving

Difficulties of congregational polity are often most visible around issues of money. Should we require minimum financial contributions from members? Which programs are funded and supported with staff? Should we have a separate fee for children in our religious education programs? Is our staff fairly compensated? What is our obligation to the UUA and the district?

We can answer these questions only if we have open discussions about money. But as a recent sociological study has found, "It doesn't matter that money, possessions, and giving are among the most common topics addressed throughout the Bible. The church in the United States has often chosen to shun the issue in practice. For example, Princeton sociologist Robert Wuthnow found that, although Americans generally avoid discussions of personal finance, it is even less common for people to talk about money among their church contacts than in other settings."[8]

Our individualism and independence lead to the attitude that no one should tell us how much we should give. Although that is our practice, a deeper understanding of mutual accountability and support would lead to more open discussions about money and the choices we make about it. Just as we expect each person to find his or her own path in spiritual development, we must each develop our balance of consumption, saving, and giving. However, as we expect to learn from one another about spirituality, we should also expect to learn from one another about financial responsibility. This exchange can only happen when we are much more open about money and how we use it.

We must also have more frank discussion among our congregations of the financial meaning of our mutual covenant. In 1994-95, 636 of 1,032 member congregations contributed at least the $32 per member Suggested Share contribution to the Annual Program Fund of the UUA. This means that more than one-third of our congregations, including some of our largest, did not meet our mutual standard, and this number has been rising. While many studies have considered other standards, such as one based on a congregation's budget instead of one based on its membership, the problem is less with the standard than with our commitment to common goals.

Even the recently adopted Rule 3.5.2, which requires congregations to contribute at least 25 percent of the Suggested Share for at least one of the last three years in order to be represented at the General Assembly, has met with some criticism.

Congregations often feel that their contributions for support of their districts and the UUA compete with the funding of their local needs, rather than viewing their contributions as serving their members and the larger world. Other congregations feel that membership in the Association should require the payment of annual dues. Some members believe that support for the UUA should only come from congregations and not from individuals, because we are an association of congregations. A clearer and more specific understanding of our polity would provide the basis for finding answers to these concerns.

Education on Stewardship

Stewardship education must be founded on a theological basis that draws on our values. Just as the covenant of our congregations informs our expectation of congregational contributions to the UUA, our shared commitment to our communities calls us to the mutual support of our congregations. Our desire for a better future demands that we invest for future generations as well.

Because member turnover is high, this educational process needs to be ongoing. Some years ago most people joining our congregations came from another denomination; today, many new members have no previous experience in a church. This means that instead of coming with an understanding of stewardship (even as a negative experience), members, especially younger ones, have little understanding of stewardship and charitable giving.

Education on stewardship must help us become responsible members of our church communities. We must connect our espoused values to the way we allocate our financial resources. The minister must develop a major part of this program, but district staff can help. The UUA has trained fundraising consultants to work in each district. However, we need additional materials such as adult education curricula to assist members in understanding a Unitarian Universalist theology of stewardship and sharing.

Before ministers are ready to educate the congregation, they must be prepared themselves. According to a study sponsored by the Lilly Endowment:

> Today's pastors are, at best, reluctant stewards of their churches' human, physical and financial resources. Although their hearts are in the right place, pastors, by their own admission, frequently lack the knowl-

New members, especially younger ones, have little understanding of stewardship and charitable giving.

edge and experience that is required to oversee the development and management of resources (people, buildings and money) that are needed to support the mission of the church. And today's seminaries, also by their own admission, are extremely reluctant to take the lead in helping pastors and other church leaders learn how to become better stewards![9]

As Unitarian Universalist seminaries have begun to grapple with this problem, the UUA, the Unitarian Universalist Ministers Association, and other UU institutions need to address the issue of continuing education on stewardship for both clergy and lay leadership. Congregations must better understand their shared responsibility for the maintenance of the UUA, their districts, theological schools, and other UU institutions. Money should cease to be a tool for gaining power and control; instead it should express our fidelity to the religious community that shares and promotes our values.

Because of the independence of member congregations, we fail to learn from one another the practices that are most likely to help congregations best serve their members and the world. Complex problems may have many solutions. We can benefit greatly from the experiences of others. The UUA and the districts could provide more information on specific topics, but the congregations own the responsibility for using the information made available.

Because of the independence of member congregations, we fail to learn from one another the practices that are most likely to help congregations best serve their members and the world.

Summary

Ministers, lay leaders, and members can benefit from renewed dialogue about their understandings of the expression of the democratic process in their congregations. Instead of developing these processes and procedures in the isolation of each congregation, we can learn from one another's experience which procedures work best. Specific areas of concern are the relations between lay leaders and ministers, the qualification and removal of members, decisions about who is authorized to speak for the congregation, and understandings of our mutual commitments and accountability.

Recommendations

1. As a guide to congregations, the UUA should make available information beyond that in *The Congregational Handbook*. Possible topics include governance, finance, personnel, administration, and computer software. Districts and congregations have already developed much useful information, and the UUA should aid in its dissemination.

2. Congregations should carefully review their decision-making processes, looking at the appropriateness of consensus and super-majority models. Where needed, they should clarify the appropriate decision-making roles for the congregation, board, and minister(s).

3. Congregations' bylaws should reserve only critical decisions to the full congregation, such as the calling of the minister(s), the approval of the annual budget, and the purchase or sale of land and buildings.

4. Congregations need to negotiate carefully with their ministers the style that makes the best use of their respective capabilities. Ministers should have a carefully drafted letter of agreement.

5. Congregations should have a well-defined policy designating who is authorized to speak on behalf of the congregation.

6. Congregations and their members should adhere to a standard of free expression without censure. However, they should also have the right of dissent. It may be desirable to allow any member of the congregation to address the gathered community from the pulpit or another forum under controlled conditions.

7. The UUA should develop recommended procedures for congregations about accepting new members, terminating membership for cause, and maintaining categories of membership.

8. Congregations should provide in their bylaws a process for terminating membership when a person's actions are contrary to the congregation's purpose and program.

9. Congregations should consider creating a Committee on Ministry to oversee the entire ministry of the congregation.

10. The UUA should make available to congregations a variety of assessment instruments and procedures for evaluating the ministry of the congregation and clergy.

11. Governance of congregations includes administration of personnel. Supervisory relationships should be clear, with written job descriptions and periodic evaluations of job performance and compensation.

12. Districts should provide opportunities for more frank discussions among our congregations of the financial meaning of our mutual covenant.

13. The UUA, the UUMA, and other UU institutions should provide opportunities for continuing education on stewardship for both clergy and lay leadership.

Sources

Interviews with Alicia Forsey, dean of continuing education and stewardship, Starr King School for the Ministry; Patti Lawrence, UUA trustee and dean of students and congregational outreach, Starr King School for the Ministry; and Fia Scheyer, former director of the UUA Annual Program Fund.

Notes

1. Lawrence X. Peers, ed, *The Congregational Handbook: How to Develop and Sustain Your Unitarian Universalist Congregation* (Boston: Unitarian Universalist Association, 1995).
2. Edwin H. Friedman, *Generation to Generation: Family Process in Church and Synagogue* (New York: Guilford Press, 1985), p. 227.
3. Brent A. Smith, "The Characteristics of Highly Effective Organizations," *First Day's Record,* Newark, Delaware, September 1995.
4. Tom Chulak, "The Free Church and Conflict-Revisited," *Unitarian Universalist Voice*, Santa Fe, New Mexico, Winter 1995, p. 9.
5. *Ibid.*, p. 10.
6. Robert T. Latham, *Committee on Ministry: A Model* (Golden, Colorado: Jefferson Unitarian Church, 1994).
7. *Ibid.*
8. Robert Wuthnow, *God and Mammon in America* (The Free Press, 1994), quoted by Johan and Sylvia Ronsvalle in "Money and Secrecy in the Church," *Congregations—The Alban Journal*, The Alban Institute, Washington, DC, November-December, 1996.
9. Dan Conway, Project Director, *The Reluctant Steward: A Report and Commentary on The Stewardship and Development Study*, co-sponsored by Christian Theological Seminary and Saint Meinrad Seminary, Indianapolis, Indiana, December 1992.

SECTION SEVEN

Cooperative Relationships

Stronger connections among congregations will strengthen "the community of autonomous congregations" that is essential to the flourishing of congregational polity within each church and throughout the movement. This section appraises the existing mechanisms for cooperation among Unitarian Universalist congregations and the needs and means to enhance these linkages, which undergird the sense of community and common cause within the overall movement.

The Unitarian Universalist Association

The organization that should provide for the widest and deepest degree of cooperative relationships among all Unitarian Universalist congregations is the Unitarian Universalist Association itself. The UUA is in an excellent position to promote, enhance, and stimulate such relationships, precisely because it was established as an association of and for all congregations in the Unitarian Universalist movement.

Some members believe, however, that the UUA has come to acquire considerably more functions and responsibilities than should be expected of an organization whose primary mission is to facilitate cooperative links among the congregations that form and largely support it. Criticism is directed, for example, to the Association's role in credentialing clergy and selecting potential candidates for referral to congregations seeking clergy as part of the settlement process. The authority of the individual congregation to call clergy of its choice is usually the most highly valued aspect of its congregational polity. Because the Association performs services like

The benefits of congregational polity for a single church do not exist in isolation, but can thrive only as part of the community of autonomous congregations.

these in connection with even this fundamental congregational decision, a significant number of Unitarian Universalists consider the UUA an overly dominant force in a movement that purports to treasure congregational polity. The people so concerned find their beliefs reinforced by the extent of UUA activities in other areas.

An overview of the present structure and operations of the UUA organization is provided in the *UUA Directory,* published annually by the Association. A copy of each edition is mailed free to every member congregation.[1] In addition to listing all congregations and ministers, the *UUA Directory* provides the names and duties of the principal officers of the UUA, and the members of its Board of Trustees, the Board's committees, and the Association's more than 50 other boards, commissions, committees, departments, offices, councils, and working groups. It also describes some 50 associate and affiliate member organizations and other denominational groups that are significant elements in the overall UU movement. The numerous positions listed in the *UUA Directory* include both elected and appointed individuals. Many of these groups and committees consist of unpaid volunteers, but paid professional staff are active throughout the organization as well.

How can the existence of such a seemingly powerful headquarters be consistent with the right of each congregation to make its own decisions, for example, the right to call its professional ministry as part of its congregational polity. See Section 4, "The UUA Bylaws: A Study in Ambivalence," for a discussion of the provisions of the Association's Bylaws on congregational polity. Despite the apparent hierarchy of the UUA, the autonomy of the congregation in calling clergy as well as in other areas is explicitly recognized in key provisions of those Bylaws.[2]

Nevertheless, some Unitarian Universalists, both new and seasoned, believe that congregational polity is endangered or negated by certain UUA offices, activities, or policies. While a few well-informed people can cite concerns that are arguable, this attitude appears primarily among the many Unitarian Universalists who are not familiar with denominational affairs.

To these people, the apparently centralized nature of some UUA operations intrudes on their congregations. A major pressure point with respect to congregational polity is thus a sense of isolation, which leads either to a lack of interest or, worse, to a sense of hostility. Both reactions result in limited or no involvement in the life of the Association and the overall movement and a narrow focus on the affairs of the individual congregation.

When a rationale for this attitude is expressed, it may be characterized as "preserving congregational polity." Yet such an interpretation does not reflect true congregational polity. A primary conclusion of this report is that the benefits of congregational polity for a single church do not exist in isolation, but can thrive *only as part of the community of autonomous*

> *A significant number of Unitarian Universalists consider the UUA an overly dominant force in a movement that purports to treasure congregational polity.*

congregations. This essential element in the concept of congregational polity is a central point emphasized by Conrad Wright.[3] His historical analysis ranges from the original seventeenth-century New England parishes through the more than 1,000 congregations in the UUA today.

How can decision making and policy setting by the one organization that can most appropriately reflect the entire community of autonomous congregations—the UUA—be carried out in new ways? The goal should be for the dubious congregations to learn that the Unitarian Universalist Association, which to them seems both authoritarian and useless, actually intrudes less and offers more help than they believe. One means of achieving this goal is through an array of measures to further decentralize many UUA services and activities into the existing UU districts and to regions or smaller groups within them.

Decentralization of Services and Activities

The Association has established 23 districts[4] in its continental organization. These include geographically compact districts with 30, 40, or 50 or more congregations each (e.g., Massachusetts Bay, with 57 congregations in part of one state; and Metropolitan New York, with 51 congregations in neighboring parts of three states), on one side of the continuum. On the other side, some districts cover very wide geographic areas and have either many or few congregations (e.g., Pacific Northwest, with 66 congregations in four states and one province; and Western Canada, with nine congregations in four provinces). Of course, the size of individual congregations also varies considerably within a given district.

Although districts are recognized in the UUA Bylaws, no specific purpose is stated for them beyond their longstanding political role, under which they elect 20 of the 25 members of the UUA Board of Trustees.[5] In more recent years, however, the development of new nomenclature has subtly helped the districts to become important vehicles for the delivery of services for member congregations.

Until a few years ago, most districts had a professional staff of only one person, a member of the Unitarian Universalist clergy or a layperson, whose official title was District Executive. There is growing recognition in the UU movement that the title "executive" is inappropriate for a community of autonomous UU churches enjoying congregational polity. In the District of Metropolitan New York, for example, the title now used is "District and Congregational Services Consultant." Other districts have taken similar steps.

Changes such as these also harmonize with the new name of the central UUA office that relates to the districts, which has been transformed from the "District Services Department" to "Department for Congregational, District, and Extension Services." Emphasizing the word "congregational" reflects the primary purpose of this department—to serve each congregation in every district. (The inclusion of Extension Services reflects a merger of two UUA departments with certain related functions.) Most professional field staff are paid jointly by the district and the UUA; each pays about half of the salary packages. This change in nomenclature helps to emphasize that it is increasingly each district's responsibility to provide key services to the congregations in the following areas.

- **Religious Education.** Under a plan initiated in 1994,[6] each district is to have available at least a part-time specialist in Unitarian Universalist religious education to provide consulting services to congregations concerned about the strength and content of their religious education programs and activities. Other specialized district-based consulting services are also emerging.

- **Inter-ethnic Relations.** Several districts or clusters within a district (including the Metro New York District and the Chicago and Oakland metropolitan areas) have experimented with using an inter-group relations consultant and other models to strengthen existing multicultural congregations.[7] These professionals must also be able to work effectively with selected congregations, first in helping them to recognize the failure to achieve full racial justice in multicultural communities where Unitarian Universalists are present, and in developing means to advance the cause of racial justice locally.

    It is important that such programs also be mounted in all-white congregations or areas to help many citizens of European descent to discover in themselves and their congregations the more subtle, and often unrecognized, elements and sources of racism, ethnocentrism, or antisemitism. The next steps must be to help the white majority of Unitarian Universalists to learn to overcome and dismantle racism in their own congregations and wider communities. Efforts such as these should also lead to greater ethnic diversity among UU church members, a goal advocated by many Unitarian Universalists and the elected leadership of the Association. See Section 11, "Marginalized Groups," for more discussion of this topic.

- **Fundraising Expertise.** Yet another kind of service to local congregations that is increasingly available through the districts is the referral of consultants on fundraising issues. Such professionals may be asked by a congregation to provide advice and guidance on strengthening techniques for the annual canvass of members. These techniques might include research on donor prospects, proposed programs for congregation-wide activities to develop consensus on and support for the needs to be met through annual pledges, and methods and materials for one-on-one visits by canvass solicitors to prospective donors at every level.

Fundraising consultants are also called on for help with capital campaign feasibility studies. The purpose is to forecast whether a proposed acquisition, improvement, expansion, or replacement of a church facility has a fair chance of financial success. Next come requests for advice on an array of techniques and procedures to solicit multiyear pledges, identifying sources of grants and loans on favorable terms, and group and individual activities and programs to develop optimum interest and support for the goal(s) chosen by the congregation. In some cases a district budget may provide a portion of the consultant's fee and expenses, but the local congregation typically must meet these costs.

- **Other New Responsibilities.** Districts are now beginning to provide assistance with ministerial transitions and advice on ministerial and staff compensation, youth programs, extension projects, leadership schools, and district-Association relations.[8] Some districts hope to add staff support as well, for implementing and coordinating social justice programs in the district and for assisting congregations that need help in this area. Districts are also adding more informational exchange sessions on new activities to their periodic business meetings and are sponsoring other special sessions, workshops, and panel discussions to help congregations learn about trends and developments in other churches, in their district and the denomination as a whole.

Decentralization and Congregational Polity

Whenever activities generated at the district level are informative and fruitful and whenever the services provided are helpful locally, the effect enhances congregational polity. The participating churches and fellowships learn from each other's successes and failures. Both nearby and distant neighbors within a district develop a stronger sense of mutual respect and trust. Actively sharing in the community of autonomous congregations deepens belief in the value of the UU movement as a whole.

The districts have the potential to foster the many types of connections we deem important. Participants in activities such as summer institutes, district meetings, cluster meetings, or sister congregation exchanges find real value in contact with people from other congregations, the exchange of ideas and approaches, and the development of personal relationships.

Districts could be more intentional about targeting affinity groups for

Actively sharing in the community of autonomous congregations deepens belief in the value of the UU movement as a whole.

these activities. Cluster meetings should be tested on topics such as congregational size or training programs, rather than mere geographic proximity. Yoking congregations together for purposes such as support, advice, social interaction, and pulpit exchanges has great potential for enhancing communication and connectedness among congregations.

Much change is happening at the district and regional levels. Districts, regions, and clusters are an increasingly important means of interconnecting congregations and the UUA, even though they were not primarily designed for that purpose. At the same time, the districts vary widely in area, number of congregations, and number of members. For these and other reasons—including uneven availability of technological equipment, resources, and staff—districts differ considerably in their ability to deliver an ideal array of services and information. Careful thought should be given to how the UUA can support the dissemination of services and information within districts and their regions so as to nurture optimally the community of autonomous congregations.[9]

We recommend that the UUA Board of Trustees request the District Presidents Council, together with other particularly knowledgeable individuals, examine all feasible steps—in full consultation with other cognizant leaders within the UUA organization, districts, and especially individual congregations—to strengthen the system of decentralized activities and services in all districts, regions, and clusters; to meet identified needs; and to report its findings and recommendations.

While such a study should help strengthen the sense of community and common cause among all participants within each district, many other congregational groups already function cooperatively without formal recognition by the UUA.

We believe that another helpful approach would be for the UUA to foster the development of joint ventures among congregational groups that have common spheres of interest and concern and/or that share physical proximity. Here are some examples of geographically defined groups and groups based on common concerns:

- Regional or metropolitan groupings, such as the Chicago or New York Metro clusters.

- Functional programs, such as the UU Urban Ministries in the Boston region (formerly The Benevolent Fraternity, founded in 1834), and the more recent Puget Sound UU Council extension effort.

- Looser groupings, such as the Partner Church Council which connects UU congregations in many districts with individual Unitarian churches in Hungary and Rumania that face much hardship. Up to $100,000 per year in aid has been provided through the Council, which is independently incorporated.[10] (See Section 12, "Internationalism," for more information about the Partner Church Council.)

- The North Texas Association of UU Societies, which has raised funds to build a 250-unit housing complex for senior citizens, staffed with a part-time nurse practitioner and a part-time social worker. The Association has also provided space for a Head Start Program. Recently, its members have enabled smaller, isolated lay-led societies to have a UU minister lead services from time to time.[11]

- The pilot project in the Joseph Priestley District, which is assuming new responsibility for the recruitment, nurture, and care of ministerial students, in cooperation with the UUA Department of Ministry staff and the Ministerial Fellowship Committee, and increasingly, with local congregations.[12]

- The undertaking by individual congregations concerned about assuring a continuing succession of clergy to provide more student internships and to help each student in seminary meet the requirement of the Ministerial Fellowship Committee that she or he be sponsored by a UU congregation.[13]

- The Coming of Age Program in the Prairie Star District, which originated in the Twin Cities area of Minnesota, has both large and small congregations participating in a series of retreats focusing on youth in their high school years (13 congregations now serve about 40 youths at any one time).[14]

- The East Michigan Growth Project, a group of eight congregations in the greater Detroit area that helps new and existing congregations to explore their growth potential, including an advertising program in the area for "The Religion That Puts Its Faith in You," and a toll-free telephone number for UU information.[15]

- The formation of Canadian Unitarians for Social Justice, spearheaded by members of Metro Toronto congregations to oppose government cuts in funds for social services.[16]

- The commitment of more than half of the UU churches in New Jersey to work together in support of the national effort of the Unitarian Universalist Service Committee to strengthen programs that protect children and enable them to develop to their full potential.[17]

- Summertime retreats at The Mountain, in Highlands, North Carolina, where multicultural congregations in major cities share experiences, problems, and growth plans. Participants have included All Souls Church, Washington, DC; Community Church of New York; First Unitarian Society, Chicago; and the UU Church of the Restoration, Philadelphia.

- Special purpose groupings for activities such as a joint ordination, a community-wide celebration, or sending truckloads of medicines to Central America under the auspices of the Unitarian Universalist Service Committee.

Congregational polity not only permits but also definitely encourages any group of congregations to act jointly by mutual agreement in any way in which congregations can act individually. The above examples show the considerable variety of cooperative programs already in place; but much more needs to be accomplished.

We recommend that the Association place greater emphasis on moving promptly toward a more consultative role to foster and nourish a wide array of cooperative undertakings among congregations.

We recommend that the Association place greater emphasis on moving promptly toward a more consultative role to foster and nourish a wide array of cooperative undertakings among congregations such as those outlined above, as part of a new effort to help Unitarian Universalists achieve a more true community of autonomous congregations. The field staff can be helpful in this effort.

Such programs may be long term, like the UU Urban Ministries, or short term, like a single celebratory event. They may be localized, like a metropolitan cluster, or intentionally international, like the Partner Church Council. While the UUA cannot and should not try to control these joint ventures, which echo the spirit of cooperation between business corporations, the Association can and should actively encourage and support them.

We recommend that the UUA assist and encourage such joint ventures in the following ways:

- Publicizing examples of successful programs by publishing articles in the *World* and *Connections*; encouraging district newsletters and *The Canadian Unitarian* to act similarly; and organizing workshops at General Assemblies to disseminate information about these programs.

- Providing facilities for communication, specifically electronic communication, among congregations, professional clergy, districts and other regions, and between the UUA and other elements of the movement at every level.

- Investing a small amount of staff time to make the new UUA Internet server much more responsive and thus encourage its wider use. Although the system that the UUA has established currently supports about 20 email lists, the creation and support of such lists has been done entirely by volunteers, which has made this work extremely slow. As new technologies, such as the Internet and videoconferencing are developed, the UUA can encourage their use by providing information and technical support. See Section 8, "Communications," for more information.

- Encouraging congregations that have created successful joint ventures to teach others how much can be achieved in this way.

Such joint ventures offer new opportunities to make productive use of the freedom and creativity that congregational polity fosters. They utilize horizontal communication networks, ad hoc organizations, and local initiatives. Joint ventures, if actively supported, can add a new dimension to congregational polity in the Unitarian Universalist movement.

The General Assembly

The General Assembly (GA) of the Unitarian Universalist Association is the major event in the yearly life of the denomination. Each congregation is entitled to select and send one or more voting delegates, depending on the number of its own members, and designate alternates as well. Ministers in Fellowship with the UUA and serving member churches are also entitled to be voting delegates.

Each year the GA Planning Committee schedules between 250 and 300 program elements during the five-day period. These include plenary business sessions, where debate and action take place on proposed Amendments to Bylaws and Rules, one UUA (US or Continental) Statement of Conscience, proposed Study/Action Issues for Social Justice, GA Actions of Immediate Witness, Business Resolutions, and other measures requiring votes; plus worship services, hearings, workshops, lectures, panel discussions, performances, social and recreational events, and meetings of all manner of associated and affiliated groups.

The General Assembly is also the venue for periodic voting in elections for certain UUA positions, including president, moderator, trustee-at-large, and members of standing committees. Provision is made for absentee election ballots for congregations that are not sending delegates to a General Assembly at which any such elections are to be held. There are no current provisions for absentee voting on Bylaw changes. (See "Participation in Voting on All Bylaw Amendments" further on in this section.)

Some congregations are represented at General Assemblies by a full complement of delegates and alternates. Some send additional members, who come

Not enough congregations participate actively in the governance of the UUA and, in particular, the General Assemblies.

as non-voting observer-participants. In recent years approximately 2,500 people of whom about 1,600 are delegates, have attended General Assemblies, as shown by the UUA General Assembly Minutes for 1992-1996.

The value of all these activities at General Assembly notwithstanding, a major problem facing our movement is that not enough congregations participate actively in the governance of the UUA and, in particular, the General Assemblies. (The same problem occurs with district annual meetings.) Of the roughly 1,000 congregations in the UUA, only about 500 have sent one or more delegates to General Assembly in recent years.

The Reverend Howell K. Lind, district and congregational services consultant for the District of Metropolitan New York, recently stated:

> The single most challenging part of working with the congregations of the Metro District is the lack of denominational connection that a number of our congregations feel toward the district and the continental movement of Unitarian Universalism. . . . [T]here is . . . a self-imposed sense of isolation and parochialism, a reluctance to enter into and participate in the larger world of our faith. . . . My experience tells me that when congregations actively support and participate in the larger world of Unitarian Universalism, they benefit greatly in every aspect of congregational life. The expanding of vision and reaching out to the larger movement on the part of congregations is the most challenging issue that hinders our Metro District from being even better and more successful than it is.[18]

Despite the potential for stimulation and a sense of real participation in the overall movement, then, quite a few congregations pay very little attention to General Assemblies. Some cannot afford to send a lay delegate or even their minister. Apparently there are other congregations whose primary concern with their own affairs is so strong that most members simply have little or no interest in the activities of the larger Unitarian Universalist movement.

Among congregations that do send one or more lay delegates and/or a minister, one or more of the following unfortunate practices often impede the General Assembly from achieving its presumed and needed role as the true voice of the denomination:

- A tendency to see the General Assembly not as a source of inspiration or help, but as a potentially unfriendly entity that must be watched carefully, lest it interfere with the independence of congregations;

- A practice of choosing lay delegates from members of the congregation who are not particularly well informed about denominational issues and procedures and who are not part of the elected leadership of the congregation, with the result that the General Assembly decision-making process does not benefit from the participation of the informed leadership of many of its own constituent bodies;

- A tendency by lay delegates and ministers alike to report only sketchily, if at all, to their congregation (or at their annual district meeting) on what transpired at the General Assembly; and

- A failure to understand that a closer relationship with the UUA through the General Assembly (or district meeting) could benefit both congregations and the wider movement.

The Value of Recovenanting

A fundamental problem underlying these failures and inadequacies is that the structure of the movement gives much authority but very few concomitant responsibilities to individual congregations. The UUA thus makes virtually no demands, but issues only requests, invitations, or advice for such vital elements as financial support; attendance at General Assemblies and district meetings by appropriate delegates; good working relationships with members of the professional ministry; and wide cooperation among congregations.

This set of circumstances could be remedied if all congregations were invited, under a measure to be adopted by the Association through its full General Assembly process, to join in recovenanting with each other and the Association. The preamble to the current statements of the UUA Principles and Purposes reads: "We, the member congregations of the Unitarian Universalist Association, covenant to affirm and promote."[19]

Covenanting, then, is how UU congregations speak with one voice on such fundamental matters as the Principles and Purposes. If all congregations were expected to join in a formal *re*covenanting process periodically—every five years, for example—as a condition for continued participation in the larger movement, such a process would help to enhance the sense of belonging to the larger movement on the part of each congregation. In addition, certain new commitments could be included in the recovenanting process to deal with such areas of responsibility as financial support, representation at General Assembly and district meetings, good ministerial relationships, and cooperation among congregations.

We recommend that the UUA Board of Trustees appoint a special committee charged with the responsibility for drafting a proposed periodic recovenanting measure for study and ultimate adoption by General As-

The structure of the movement gives much authority but very few concomitant responsibilities to individual congregations.

sembly; and for proposing appropriate ceremonies by which each congregation would be asked, after voting to recovenant with the commitments we suggest, to record and celebrate its joinder in the recovenanting process.

Participation in Voting on All Bylaw Amendments

Because the Bylaws of the Association constitute a basic document governing congregational polity as well as setting forth the UUA Principles and Purposes and its structure and procedures, the process for changing the Bylaws is particularly pertinent to the nature and health of congregational polity. The Bylaws are continually evolving: one or more amendments are proposed at nearly every General Assembly. For example, in 1996, major changes were made in the way General Resolutions (renamed "Statements of Conscience") and other policy declarations are reviewed and revised at every stage of their development.

Most individual Bylaws may be amended by a two-thirds vote at any General Assembly. Others, designated C-Bylaws, can be changed only by passage at two General Assemblies, first by a majority vote and then by a two-thirds vote. The designation "C-Bylaws" was made at the time of merger in 1961, presumably because of the fundamental nature of these provisions. C-Bylaws govern such matters (among others) as the statements of Principles and Purposes, non-discrimination, and freedom of belief;[20] member societies, congregational polity, admission to membership, and termination of membership;[21] the annual General Assembly;[22] responsibilities of the Board of Trustees;[23] raising of funds and responsibility for investments;[24] ministerial fellowship;[25] Districts and their autonomy;[26] and amendments to the Bylaws.[27]

Because of the Association's commitment to the democratic process, each congregation should participate in the adoption of all changes in the fundamental document of the Association. Such provision would be also consistent with the election process, which permits casting absentee ballots in election years as well as voting by the delegates at General Assembly.

We recommend that an amendment to the Bylaws be drafted by counsel to provide that all future amendments be adopted by a two-year process. The first year would be a non-election year and the amendment would be adopted at the General Assembly by majority vote. The second year would be an election year, and the amendment would be placed on the election ballot. Passage would require a two-thirds approval of the votes cast, including those voted absentee.

Once adopted, this procedure would enable all UU congregations to have a say in any amendments that might even remotely affect their polity and in all other changes in UUA governance and procedure. It would eliminate the somewhat arbitrary distinction between C-Bylaws and other bylaws. By synchronizing this measure and all future proposed amendments with the UUA elections that are held only in alternate years, the added cost of mailing materials on proposed amendments would be negligible.

We recognize that this change would cause the amendment of what are now non-C-Bylaws to take a year longer, but we believe that being more deliberate in the alteration of the Association's basic document would have significant advantages. The process we propose would provide an opportunity for the almost 500 congregations that are not now represented at General Assemblies to be included in voting on every proposed amendment to the basic document that governs all congregations. This change would enhance the connections among all congregations and be more consistent with the Principles and Purposes of the Unitarian Universalist movement. The interest generated in proposed amendments might help to stimulate more congregations to be represented at General Assembly.

Summary

The benefits of congregational polity for a single church cannot be fully enjoyed in isolation, for true congregational polity can thrive *only as part of the community of autonomous congregations*. Our goal should be to help dubious congregations learn that the seemingly distant yet intrusive UUA actually intrudes less than they believe and offers many kinds of useful assistance to their congregations that should be seen as beneficial and should be fully utilized.

A major means to make such services better understood and appreciated is to increase substantially their delivery on a decentralized basis to each district and its regions or clusters. At the same time, efforts should be made to encourage the development of additional cooperative ventures among congregations that are either geographically based or that focus on common concerns.

The General Assembly and district meetings also need changes to attract participation of a significantly larger percentage of congregations and their leadership. To help assure that each congregation meets its responsibilities to the larger movement, a process for periodic recovenanting by all with each other should be devised and implemented.

To provide a greater role in UUA decision making for congregations that do not now send delegates to General Assemblies, the Bylaws should be amended to make all future amendments subject to approval by two General Assemblies. All changes will first be approved by a majority vote at a General Assembly. They will also require a two-thirds vote at the sec-

Our goal should be to help dubious congregations learn that the seemingly distant yet intrusive UUA actually offers many kinds of useful assistance to congregations.

ond GA coinciding with elections, including absentee ballots. This will permit participation by those congregations unable to attend, as they are now included in voting for elected positions that form the leadership of the movement.

Recommendations

1. The Board of Trustees should request the District Presidents Council to recommend specific measures to further decentralize to districts—and to regions or clusters within them—more services, functions, and responsibilities, through the means specified above in the full text of this recommendation.

2. The Association should move promptly toward a more consultative role to foster and nourish a wide array of cooperative undertakings among congregations, without regard to geographic proximity. The Association should assist and encourage such joint ventures by means of specific proposals set forth above in the full text of this recommendation.

3. The Board of Trustees should appoint a special committee charged with the responsibility for drafting a proposed periodic recovenanting measure for study and ultimate adoption by the 1998 and 1999 General Assemblies. This committee should also propose appropriate ceremonies by which each congregation would be asked, after voting to recovenant with the commitments we suggest above in the full text of this recommendation, to record and celebrate its joinder in the recovenanting process.

4. An amendment to the Bylaws should be drafted to make all Bylaw changes subject to a two-year process, the second of which would coincide with elections and would permit absentee voting on the amendment.

Sources

The following were consulted (as were many fellow members of the Commission on Appraisal): Jerry Davidoff and Edward Leibensberger, general counsel to the UUA, and Barbara Prairie, General Assembly administrator.

Notes

1. Copies may also be purchased from the UUA Bookstore, 25 Beacon Street, Boston, Massachusetts 02108.
2. See especially *Bylaws*, Article III, "Membership," Section C-3.2, "Congregational Polity."
3. Conrad Wright, *Walking Together* (Boston: Skinner House Books, 1989).
4. See map, congregational listings, and statistics, *1996-97 UUA Directory*, pp. 36-45.
5. *Bylaws*, Article VI, "Board of Trustees," Section 6.3, "Membership."
6. The pilot program was tested in the Metropolitan New York District, beginning in 1992.
7. The initiation of this service was among several extension projects supported by a Veatch Program grant beginning in 1992.
8. See Note 7 for the funding source and timing of many of these initiatives.
9. One seemingly simple approach to ameliorate these inequalities might be to redraw district boundaries to make them more balanced, but previous attempts along this line proved inadequate.
10. The Reverend Dr. C. Leon Hopper, Jr., at Commission on Appraisal General Assembly Workshop, June 23, 1996.
11. Marty Robinson, General Assembly Workshop, June 23, 1996.
12. The Reverend Roberta O. Finkelstein, General Assembly Workshop, June 23, 1996.
13. This requirement took effect September 1, 1992.
14. Carole Martignacco, General Assembly Workshop, June 23, 1996.
15. The Reverend Carol Ann Huston, General Assembly Workshop, June 23, 1996.
16. *The Canadian Unitarian* (Toronto: Canadian Unitarian Council, May 1996), p. 4.
17. *The District DRUMMER* (Shoreham, New York: Unitarian Universalist Metro District of New York, Spring 1996), p. 2.
18. The Reverend Howell K. Lind, in *The District DRUMMER*, Fall 1996, p.2.
19. *Bylaws*, Article II, Section C-2.1.
20. *Ibid.*, Article II.
21. *Ibid.*, Article III.
22. *Ibid.*, Article IV.
23. *Ibid.*, Article VI.
24. *Ibid.*, Article X.
25. *Ibid.*, Article XI.
26. *Ibid.*, Article XII.
27. *Ibid.*, Article XIV.

SECTION EIGHT

Communications

To be a "community of autonomous churches," we must communicate with one another and we must have the mechanisms available to do so. We have a responsibility—both within and among congregations—to be informed and to inform, to share resources, and to participate in our common associational life. Yet many of our linkages appear weak or nonexistent. In addition, an informed constituency is necessary to maintain a balance of power in our congregations, districts, and Association. This section contrasts the more unified use of print media of the past with the more fragmented communication structures of the present, and makes recommendations for widening our communications base and enhancing connections through publications and video and computer technology.

In the book *Habits of the Heart*, the authors define community as "a group of people who are socially interdependent, who participate together in discussion and decision making, and who share certain practices that both define the community and are nurtured by it."[1] When the community is one of congregations, establishing avenues and habits of communication is particularly difficult but no less critical for the definition and nurturance of the community. Although many of our congregations share certain defining practices, our interdependent linkages appear weak or, in many cases, nonexistent.

Because we do not practice a pure form of congregational polity, but have some functions and powers vested in a common body that serves us—the Unitarian Universalist Association—the question becomes, What functions can best be performed by this body? Many areas of communication fall within this category.

The effectiveness and extent of our communications determine to a great extent our ability to carry out our religious principles.

The effectiveness and extent of our communications determines to a great extent our ability to carry out our religious principles. Poor communication—inadequate information, misinformation, or a lack of substantive discourse—causes or contributes to many of our conflicts, struggles, and failures. In many cases when we attempt to inform and engage individuals and congregations, such attempts go unread. Some of us protest that we are not informed, and yet some fellowships without professional leadership complain of feeling deluged by mail from 25 Beacon Street.

With our tradition of autonomy comes a responsibility to the whole body. We have tended to focus on our independence, but it is the relational aspects of our common life that have the potential to transform us, bringing wholeness, unity, and an experience of the holy that we seek.

A Print-based Society

Until recently, we communicated either orally or through print. Our predecessors had access to information about important issues of the day through newspapers, journals, and magazines. The Unitarians had weekly newspapers in the *Christian Register* and the *Liberal Christian,* and monthly magazines such as the *Monthly Religious Magazine, Christian Examiner,* and the *Monthly Journal* of the American Unitarian Association. The Universalists had such periodicals as the *Universalist Magazine* (which went through numerous name changes), *Christian Freeman, Universalist Herald, Ladies Repository,* and the *Myrtle.* In addition, the Unitarian National Conference published reports of its meetings. Any member who wanted to keep abreast of issues had access to an enormous amount of information. Controversial statements or reports would produce quick responses and rebuttals. In short, there was a common forum for addressing the concerns of the denominations, clarifying issues, and reaching some measure of agreement.

Present Communications: Reading Between the Lines

Our communication structures are oldstyle and hierarchical, with information flowing down from the UUA and districts to congregations.

These are difficult times for print media. Radio, then television, have in large measure replaced newspapers and magazines in the general population. Because of costs, our relatively small size, financial constraints, or perhaps the lack of a strong organization, our Association has failed to use the electronic media to any significant extent. We have made a few attempts to utilize radio, television, and videotaping and are beginning to develop networks for computer-assisted communications.

At the same time, our official publications have dwindled to a very few. Some of these have a definite public relations slant or are targeted to a narrow audience and are inadequate channels for furthering our dialogue. Independent publications have suffered from a lack of funding and general support. For example, we have seen the demise of *Kairos* and *Journal of the Liberal Ministry*.

Our congregations are isolated from one another, with no expectations of significant relationships and exchanges of resources among congregations. To a large extent, our communication structures are oldstyle and hierarchical, with information flowing down from the UUA and districts to congregations. Although congregations are encouraged first to approach districts rather than the UUA for assistance, there is tremendous variability in district capabilities to deliver information and services and no consistency among district offices in terms of technology and delivery systems.

Looking Ahead

As part of its work, the Commission on Appraisal holds open hearings around the country and meets with staff and constituent groups. One of the continuing themes of our discussions is the frustration that members feel about the lack of connection with and knowledge of the wider movement. We hear this concern variously expressed as apathy, provincialism, rugged individualism, and isolation. We duplicate efforts by not sharing resources, often because we either don't know they exist or don't know how to secure the help we need.

We duplicate efforts by not sharing resources, often because we either don't know they exist or don't know how to secure the help we need.

Our culture has made a radical shift in communication styles with the availability of electronic communications, from traditional top-down systems to a many-to-many system of communicating, with information flowing laterally as well as hierarchically. The potential for congregations to be more informed, connected, and served is tremendous. Acknowledging the value of all types of communication, we will limit our discussion here to more formalized communication avenues and not address the issues of interpersonal communications or public relations.

The Association's Publications

The Association produces the *World* magazine, *Ethics and Action*, a REACH packet for religious education, Department of Ministry packets, and *Connections*. The Association also designs and publishes materials for the Pamphlet Commission. The Canadian Unitarian Council publishes the *Canadian Unitarian*. Independent publications of note are *First Day's Record*, *Unitarian Universalist Voice*, and *The Unitarian Universalist Christian*. Because of budget constraints and the rising cost of printed materials, new print publications are not likely to be developed. We need to ask how congregations can improve communications through existing publications and how they can benefit more from them.

One answer is more dialogue between the UUA and congregations about who should receive various publications, both individuals and groups. In addition, UUA publications, which are now strictly products of the Association, could include more input from other Unitarian Universalists and more exchanges between congregations and members. We believe that broadening the base of the editorial board of the *World* magazine to include more non-staff members would enhance its appeal and widen its perspective. According to former editor Linda Beyer McHugh, the *World* is about to expand its advisory board beyond UU staff. McHugh feels that an expanded travel budget for the *World* would also improve the staff's ability to cover stories around the continent.

Part of the stated mission of the *World* conveys what we as a Commission envision for our movement:

> The *World* seeks to develop the broad denominational picture by articulating Unitarian Universalist values, purposes, and spirituality . . . promoting denominational self-reflection and understanding by making known UU activities, personalities, and history.

Addressing the issue of simply providing more information, McHugh adds, "It's a fantasy to think a newspaper can enhance our communication just by publishing everything. What we need, instead, is careful editing."

She says that new UU members are the magazine's primary audience, but that the *World* tries to attend to the needs and interests of all groups and to long-standing Unitarian Universalists as well. For example, McHugh adds, "With the themed issues, we can do lots on different levels to meet different needs." The addition in 1996 of the section "Congregational Life and Leadership" has the potential to meet our stated goal of enhancing our connection to other congregations and promoting interrelatedness. We commend the *World* and support the expansion of such a section beyond its current size.

At present, the process for adding new members to the subscription list for the *World* is manual and slow, making it hard to reach new members at a time when they most want information about Unitarian Universalism. This process could be done easily and quickly by computer, at least for our larger congregations, which contain most of our members. According to Steve Buccieri, former director of information services, the UUA recently purchased a database program that can compare Association files with individual church databases. We encourage the speedy automatization of this process.

Although we will not address in this report Beacon Press and Skinner House publications, we recognize the tremendous contribution they make in promoting UU values and identity. We would like to see on the copyright pages more prominent mention of the Association, for example, wording such as "Beacon Press—committed to the values of Unitarian Universalism," as well as the wider marketing of Skinner House books through commercial bookstores.

Unitarian Universalist Advance, an independent organization, launched its journal *UU Voice* in 1994 to provide a forum for discourse beyond a house organ. The Reverend Dr. Brent Smith, former editor, believes that the role of the journal is to increase the number of voices in communication. "There is a relationship between the strength of autonomous congregations and the multiple variety of forms of communication. To fulfill our role as autonomous congregations demands we have a variety of different communication vehicles," Smith states.

Smith believes that our recent practices are becoming denominational rather than associational, with more centralization and consolidation. "I see a whole generation of ministers working in that centralized environment. With the *UU Voice*, we are concerned with the preservation of the free press and the free spirit. We want to hear many voices. Our interest is not in critiquing the UUA. We are focused on individual autonomous congregations."

Two Examples of Video Production

The experiences of two of our congregations with video broadcasting highlight many issues of polity and connectedness.

Since 1974, All Souls Unitarian Church in Tulsa, Oklahoma, has engaged in a broadcast ministry. The Reverend Dr. John Wolf, minister emeritus, comments that being a congregation in the same city with Oral Roberts positioned it for a television ministry: "Oral Roberts was a pioneer of electronic religion. He blazed a trail. He also created a need for others to counteract his message." All Souls, Tulsa, was also fortunate to have a congregant, Rocky Stegman, who was willing to make broadcast programs through his production company and to donate his services. Costing the church nothing for the first five or six years, the broadcast ministry in later years cost about $3,000 per segment for 26 segments produced each year. According to Wolf and to Dr. Brent Smith, senior minister, "Univision," which later became "Faith and the Free Church" very successfully accomplished its goal of promoting religious freedom.

In the 1980s they were encouraged to nationalize the program. According to Smith, the Association was in a push to solidify power in the national organization. The program's advisory committee decided that the focus was to represent various viewpoints, where Tulsa's mission had been to promote religious freedom. The production was moved to Atlanta, acquired a national director, produced one episode that cost in excess of $100,000, and the project failed. The production later returned to Tulsa, but lost the name "Univision" in the process. In recent years the program has been broadcast on the "Religion and Values" channel, which presents a variety of religious perspectives.

Smith says, "The channel loved us, because we were the only ones doing religious programs, as opposed to dealing primarily with social justice topics." The programs aired on the local religious channel five times each weekend. Viewing the programs as mission work for other congregations in the Association, the church produced short commercials for other congregations to use as lead-ins when they aired the segments in their local markets. Production, which halted in 1996 after a serious illness of the producer, was scheduled to resume in 1997.

The Unitarian Universalist Church of Rockford, Illinois, now has a library of 380 segments of its "Fusion" program after 15 seasons. The Reverend David Weissbard, senior minister, says he effectively has 4,000 people in his "congregation" because of the large viewing audience. "Given the right-wing times we live in, how can we not do it," reflected Weissbard. "It's community ministry."

The program, which costs about $500 per segment to produce, has never been fully funded from the church's operating budget, but receives some support from endowment funds and other outside gifts. Weissbard says that there has never been unanimous support for funding the program within the Rockford congregation, but that there is strong support for the program's ministry.

According to Weissbard, the production costs are reasonable because Rockford is a small television market and the production rates are lower. Taping occurs in a local television studio. Airing after "CBS Sunday Morning," "Fusion" benefits from some carryover audience. Some of the segments also have been used for Sunday programming by fellowships without professional leadership.

Weissbard cites the opportunity to articulate the congregation's positions and issues and to have a panel of church members respond to the sermons to demonstrate Unitarian Universalist support for differing opinions. Weissbard has heard from people of color that they are not comfortable attending a predominantly white church but appreciate the content of the programs through television access.

For 10 of the segments each year, other UU ministers tape sermons for "Fusion" and stay overnight to preach for the Rockford congregation. The Reverend Weissbard believes that the congregation benefits from having so many ministers in the pulpit and that members feel a stronger connection to other congregations and to Unitarian Universalism as a result.

Only recently have these two productions received any funding from the UUA, and then only sporadically. Yet both producers believe that they are generating programs that are relevant and useful for the entire Association, and at a lower cost than a large market such as Boston would incur.

Partnerships among districts, the UUA, and congregations or clusters of congregations to provide products and services such as video segments, religious education courses, and church administration courses could be beneficial to all parties. Video technology may be a viable way to promote congregational interest and participation in General Assemblies as well. The GA Planning Comittee and staff could help by commissioning the creation of a video about General Assembly, to be made available to all congregations.

Will We Move Into the Electronic Age?

The UUA is developing a site on the World Wide Web almost entirely with the help of volunteers. Efforts thus far have focused on setting up a high speed connection from UUA headquarters to the Internet. The potential for electronic communications is immense. Among the possibilities are directed email; communications within districts and clusters on a variety of topics; linking congregations by various criteria; reporting on events and issues; running discussion groups; sharing ministerial, editorial, and congregational resources; publishing committee and board reports and minutes; providing information about settlements, openings, milestones, and passages; and faxing via computer modems.

By early March 1996, more than 100 UU congregations had home pages on the Internet, many of very high quality. The cost of creating home pages is reasonable. Many committees, districts, and the UUA Board of Trustees are communicating through email. An email list for UUA announcements, duplicated on the UUA web page, was recently begun under the auspices of the Public Relations, Marketing, and Information Office. The UUA Committee on Technology and Electronic Communications outlined to the board the potential uses of electronic communications by the Association. Having met its original charge, the committee in a report to the board dated January 1996 suggested work yet to be done. The Board of Trustees has since charged a new committee with this work.

The Internet creates the ability for dialogue to occur among a wide variety of interest groups, resulting in the decentralization of information, responsibility, and power. Both moderated and unmoderated discussions are possible. CD-ROM technology provides an inexpensive way to distribute

We let the age of television pass us by. If we don't get busy, we'll miss the electronic age as well!

masses of information, with costs in the $1 to $2 range per CD for production and inexpensive mailing. With lower costs than printed matter, CD-ROMs would be especially practical for the distribution of bulky materials such as the *UUA Directory*, *The Congregational Handbook*, General Assembly reports and information, and Commission on Appraisal reports. The flexibility afforded by CD-ROMs is advantageous, with the ability to store pictures, sound, and video as well as text.

The UUA is the logical body to provide staff to coordinate and manage the electronic communication system and to provide a database librarian. Such a system should ultimately free staff members from disseminating information to attend to other areas of need. The UUA plans to add a part-time staff person as a librarian to facilitate making information accessible via the Internet. According to former director of information services Steve Buccieri, there is a recommendation as well to add a part-time technical support position in the Information Services Department. As Buccieri comments, "The work that has been done so far primarily by volunteers is commendable, but it could use some professional midwifing." Adding these two staff positions has the potential for making information on a variety of topics available quickly and at low cost. Examples of appropriate applications range from the *Ministerial Settlement Handbook* to social justice materials such as the *Resolutions and Resources Handbook*.

A Shift in Managing Information

Rather than having information flowing to and from headquarters, the emphasis would be on managing and directing the flow of information among congregations.

Such a shift in information management is radical. Rather than having information flowing to and from headquarters, the emphasis would be on managing and directing the flow of information *among* congregations, staff departments, and affinity groups. However, formulating thoughtful policies and practices for this type of information management requires substantial lead time. As the Reverend John Wolf says, "We let the age of television pass us by. If we don't get busy, we'll miss the electronic age as well!"

The start-up stage of computerization within our association poses inherent—but not insurmountable—problems, because some of our congregations do not have computers, although at least one member of each congregation almost certainly does. Moving into the electronic age also raises new questions: How does information get disseminated? Who holds the information (and thus the power)? How available is this information to the general membership? The process of answering these questions is important as well.

Our goal is to encourage greater participation in associational life and to use and make available all possible resources to strengthen our common community while honoring our tradition of congregational autonomy and authority over local affairs. A broad view of congregational polity suggests that information and resources developed in our individual congregations be made available to all of our congregations.

Summary

Building a truly interdependent web of congregations, districts, and the Unitarian Universalist Association is virtually impossible without communication avenues and sytems that are widely available, inexpensive, informative, and accessible. Communication is the foundation of the community of congregations implied by a broader understanding of polity. Efforts to date to enhance and expand our base of communications—through print, video, CD-ROM, and electronic technology—have been limited, although we have several successful prototypes. The shift in information management will require significant lead time and planning as well as new staff positions and more money.

Recommendations

1. The editorial board of the *World* should be broadened to enhance its appeal and widen its perspective.

2. We commend the increased coverage of congregational life and issues in the *World* and support the expansion of this section in the future.

3. The mailing list for the *World* should be updated monthly using the Association's new database software.

4. We encourage financial support for independent, non-house publications, either through the UUA budget or grants.

5. We commend Beacon Press and Skinner House Books and we recommend that our connection with Beacon Press be made more public, and that Skinner House Books be marketed more broadly.

6. The use of video, radio, and local access television by congregations and the denomination should be encouraged and supported by the Association and shared among congregations.

7. We recommend adding staff positions for a database librarian and

for a technical support person to help congregations share resources and promote Unitarian Universalism in the larger community.

Sources

Interviews with Linda Beyer McHugh, former editor, the *World*; Brent A. Smith, former editor, *Unitarian Universalist Voice,* and senior minister, All Souls Unitarian Church, Tulsa, Oklahoma; John B. Wolf, minister emeritus, All Souls Unitarian Church, Tulsa, Oklahoma; David R. Weissbard, senior minister, the Unitarian Universalist Church, Rockford, Illinois; Robert T. Snow, vice president for development, Unitarian Universalist Association; and Steve Buccieri, former director of information services, Unitarian Universalist Association.

Note

1. Robert N. Bellah, Richard Madsen, William M. Sullivan, Ann Swidler, and Steven M. Tipton, *Habits of the Heart* (Berkeley: University of California Press, 1985), p. 333.

SECTION NINE

Religious Leadership

Religious leadership at the congregational level is a key area in which different understandings of congregational polity create difficulties within our Association. We have a wide variety of approaches to leadership, from ordained clergy through volunteer lay members of a congregation, who may also be ordained or commissioned, elected or not. At every level, the understanding of congregational polity is crucial to what we do. Not only must we have good leadership to survive and thrive—our system and style of leadership must be undergirded by a clear understanding of what it means to be congregational so that our approach in governing and running our congregations is consistent with the broader reach of Unitarian Universalism. This section views issues of religious leadership through the lens of congregational polity and makes recommendations for strengthening leadership in the following: categories of ministry, shared ministry, recruitment and formation of ministerial students, ordination, and community ministry.

The presence of educated, trained, and dedicated ordained clergy has long been central to our existence. Even lay-led congregations recognize that having such clergy within the Association is necessary to keep us strong and viable. For years, parish-based clergy were the only formally recognized ministers within the Association and became the expected standard. However, during the 1960s and 1970s we became aware of the specialized requirements that ministry of religious education demanded. In response to studies and a vote at General Assembly, in 1980 the Ministerial Fellowship Committee (MFC) began granting Fellowship as ministers of religious education.

To affirm the fact that we have one professional ministry, we recommend abolishing the separate categories of parish, religious education, and community ministry.

Additionally, in the 1980s and 1990s we came to understand the special call to ministry outside the walls of our congregations. Again in response to a vote at General Assembly, the MFC began granting Fellowship as community ministers in 1991. Recognition of the special nature of the work of these clergy is important. One category of community ministry presently covers a wide variety of specializations such as ministry to youth, chaplaincies in hospitals and prisons, community organizing, and a wide variety of other work.

Abolishing Categories of Ministry

The presence of these three categories (parish ministers, ministers of religious education, and community ministers) fosters the perception that the parish ministers are the "real" ministers and that the other two categories of ministry require less ability and skill. This misconception is understandable in that parish ministers are often the most visible ministers in any congregation. Yet ministers of religious education and community ministers must not only meet the same criteria of training, skill, and ability as parish ministers, but must also demonstrate an understanding of their area of specialization. The preparation for any form of Unitarian Universalist ministry is challenging and demanding and the categories of ministry seek only to recognize areas of specialization.

To affirm the fact that we have one professional ministry, we recommend abolishing the separate categories of parish, religious education, and community ministry. Ministers should be received into Ministerial Fellowship with the potential for adding areas of specialization. This proposal is similar to the system of credentialing doctors—all are subject to the same basic criteria, but may achieve additional certification in specific areas. This plan would ensure that all clergy have the basic skills needed to relate to congregational structure (such as preaching, interpersonal communication, and knowledge of history, theology, and polity), as well as the skills relevant to their chosen form of ministry. The Ministerial Fellowship Committee would define the areas of specialization and establish requirements for experience and education in these areas.

We foresee the possibility of having many areas of specialization, whenever criteria for education and experience can be defined. These areas might include ministry to youth, ministry to young adults, campus ministry, prison chaplaincy, ministry to the dying, AIDS ministry, interim ministry, and ministry of music. Specialization would enable congregations or other potential employers to select people with certification in the required skills, rather than trying to determine the specifics about each person.[1]

Ministerial Membership Requirement

Congregations are both the lifeblood of our religious movement and the place where we build and maintain our relationships with each other as religious people. Clergy, regardless of the setting of their ministry, are ministers "of the church," called from its ranks. We are Unitarian Universalists through affiliation with a congregation, not through adherence to a particular set of views or by undergoing a particular sacrament. Indeed, only as a member of a Unitarian Universalist congregation can a minister truly claim a UU identity, since our movement is an association of congregations. Therefore, all clergy, regardless of where they serve, should be active members of a Unitarian Universalist congregation. (Exception must be made for ministers holding dual standing in another religious tradition where that tradition's rules may prohibit such membership.) The authenticity and credibility of ministers will only be enhanced if they are active members of the religious movement from which they minister.

The authenticity and credibility of ministers will only be enhanced if they are active members of the religious movement from which they minister.

Shared Ministry

One key aspect of Unitarian Universalism is our belief that ministry of the congregation does not belong exclusively to ordained clergy, but to everyone. In *Our Professional Ministry: Structure, Support and Renewal*, the Commission's 1992 study, Neil Shadle stated, "Ministry is the vocation of every person of faith, [and] Unitarian Universalism, as a democratic faith, affirms the 'priesthood of all believers'; we are all lay ministers, whether or not we choose to be professional religious leaders."[2] This belief in the "priesthood of all believers" is central to who we are as a religious movement.

Not only does shared ministry refer to ministry shared between professional clergy in multi-staff settings, but also to ministry shared between professional ministers and laypeople. Good relationships between colleagues in a multi-staff setting provide models of collaboration and trust that can help congregations articulate a vision of shared ministry across professional and lay lines. Publications such as *The Shared Ministry Sourcebook*[3] begin to deepen the conversation about how this shared lay and professional ministry could look. To enhance our understanding of what shared ministry is and could be, we recommend that congregations enter into wide-ranging conversations at the area and district levels about common goals that should undergird lay ministry.

These conversations are necessary for several reasons. As the results of the 1993 UUA Women and Religion survey show, we lack consensus about the shape and nature of lay ministry within our congregations. Shared ministry is seen to range from "the minimal participation of lay persons as 'helpers' or substitutes when the minister is away to formal programs involving title lay positions, training, and accreditation." The study noted that those who support shared ministry recognize the necessity for all people to work together for the health of the congregation. Those who are sceptical worry about "quality control," the boundaries that differentiate ministering from other relationships, and the potential of volunteer burnout.[4] It is this diversity of understanding and these concerns that lead to our recommendation for wide-ranging conversations.

Examples of Shared Ministry Programs

Frequently volunteers are not subject to adequate screening, training, and supervision while they are involved in lay ministry.

These conversations should take into account successful programs of shared leadership that are under way in our communities. For example, in the Associates Program at the First Unitarian Church in Oakland, California, church members help plan and assist with worship and provide pastoral care for the congregation. Programs are under development in which congregants will work with the religious education program as teachers and as social justice advocates within the church and the larger community. Volunteers are screened, trained, and supervised, and are held to high standards set by the congregation. In Bedford, Massachusetts, and Morristown, New Jersey, congregations have adapted the Oakland Worship Associates program. These spin-off programs are reportedly doing well and contributing to the vitality of the congregations.

Within Canadian congregations, the lay chaplaincy program has been active since 1970, when Unitarian (as they are often called in Canada) clergy were few and spread thinly across the nation. Two or sometimes three members of each congregation are empowered by provincial governments to perform rites of passage such as weddings, funeral and memorial services, and child dedications. (Technically, only weddings require the licensure of provincial authorities.) Congregations recruit and train their chaplains, whose appointments are overseen by the Canadian Unitarian Council.

Responsibility for training and supervision of the lay chaplains varies among congregations. Professional ministers are typically responsible for training and often supervision of chaplains in their congregations. In other cases such as lay-led congregations, the congregation's governing board oversees the chaplaincy program. In recent years, the Chaplains Association has established training programs for newer chaplains, but given the country's wide expanse and the relatively small number of congregations, not all chaplains are able to attend such training. The Chaplains Association has also established a code of ethics and conduct, which has been approved by the Ministers and Chaplains Committee of the Canadian Unitarian Council.

Other congregations have varying roles for lay leaders—from serving as trustees or directors on boards to working as deacons within the congregation. These are all viable areas of church ministry and can greatly assist the work of the called clergy.

Frequently, however, volunteers are not subject to adequate screening, training, and supervision while they are involved in lay ministry. We recommend that congregations work with their districts to define and clarify the roles and responsibilities of lay ministers. Such details as the nature of the ministry, the appropriate training required, the method of accountability to the congregation, the relationship between lay ministers and ordained clergy, the length of term, the procedures for evaluation, and the system for recognizing and commissioning such individuals should be clarified before a congregation begins a lay ministry program. Once such decisions are made, districts or area groups can collaborate on the implementation of the program. Such guidelines and training programs would greatly enhance the "priesthood of all believers."

Recruitment and Formation of Ministerial Students

Although committed laypeople donate many hours and much skill and talent to the Association, well-prepared professional clergy are necessary to perform the amount of work required to keep Unitarian Universalism a viable religious movement. To ensure that clergy maintain high standards of excellence, it is incumbent upon the Association to have the best candidates with the best preparation for professional ministry.

As recommended in the Commission on Appraisal's earlier report, *Our Professional Ministry*, we believe that congregations and the Association should work together in both the recruitment of individuals for ministry and the formation of those individuals.[5] In recruitment efforts, we urge congregations to look to people in their midst and to encourage those with the requisite skills and talents to consider the UU ministry as a career choice. Particular care should be taken to recruit those who understand our broader movement and are committed to the principles of the UUA, as well as people who can work well with the theological diversity within our congregations.

In 1992, a change was made to help strengthen the system of assisting candidates for the ministry and to help congregations be more active in the preparation and development of candidates: Any person seeking UU Fellowship must now be sponsored by a Unitarian Universalist congregation, which formulates its own selection criteria. This sponsorship may be moral, emotional, and economic, but as a bottom line, the congregation must state that it has faith in the person's ability to become a competent clergyperson. As this program is relatively new, many (if not most) congregations have not yet been faced with the decision-making process for sponsorship.

We recommend that the UUA Department of Ministry formulate standards and guidelines that congregations can use in making sponsorship decisions. These guidelines would address the qualities, skills, abilities, and commitment to calling deemed essential in a paid professional minister. Such guidelines should include not only a process for assessing the suitability of candidates for sponsorship, but also for assisting congregations in rejecting individuals they believe would not be suitable for ordained ministry. District field staff could aid congregations in the process. Congregations should review and adopt the criteria for sponsorship (based on the UUA guidelines) before any person comes to them requesting sponsorship.

Congregations must also examine the question of financial support for their ministerial candidates. With educational costs rising, new ministers often find themselves buried in debt. Congregations must take responsibility for financial assistance to the clergy of the next generation.

In-care Programs

Candidates for ministry also deserve more ongoing support and evaluation from our movement. The Department of Ministry is working with two pilot projects to provide good models—one started by clergy in the Joseph Priestley District and the other a joint effort of the Florida, Mid-South, and Thomas Jefferson Districts. These projects bring together laypeople, ordained clergy, and ministerial candidates. The goal is twofold: to provide candidates for ministry with support and guidance and to help members of congregations assume responsibility to such students. Although a support committee would not be charged with the job of telling candidates they are not suitable for ministry, it is hoped that by working together in a spirit of love, committee members can help candidates uncover their own gifts and discern whether the UU ministry is an appropriate place for them. Such a process, which incorporates retreats and other interactive methods, helps the committees, districts, clergy, and candidates to realize that they are all serving a higher purpose than a person's desire to minister; they are working together to enhance the UU movement.[6]

We commend the work of the Department of Ministry in setting up pilot programs that will help congregations do the difficult work of informing candidates when they do not measure up. To date, the bad-news telling has been left to the Fellowship Committee, but if we are to take our system of congregational polity seriously, congregations, clergy, and the Association must all play their part in the discernment process.

These changes in the formation process are too recent to be evaluated. However, if our congregations assume their responsibility for and to potential professional ministers, both in sponsoring self-selected candidates and encouraging others who may be appropriate for our ministry, they will support and enhance the work of the Fellowship Committee. Furthermore, projects like those in the Joseph Priestley District and the Florida, Mid-South, and Thomas Jefferson Districts also increase congregation's investment in the ordained ministry and their understanding of the theological underpinning of ordination.

In addition to the assistance provided by congregations, districts, and the Unitarian Universalist Association, the Panel on Theological Education also provides assistance in administering the expenditure of income from an endowment for theological education from the Unitarian Universalist Congregation at Shelter Rock, in Manhasset, New York. This income is the only financial support that the UUA provides to UU theological schools. Increasingly these funds are viewed as a source of support for many competing educational ventures. We recommend that the basic needs of Meadville/Lombard Theological School and Starr King School for the Ministry continue to be given priority in funding decisions by the Panel on Theological Education.

The Panel on Theological Education should continue to advocate for students at non-Unitarian Universalist theological schools to encourage these schools to offer students the broad range of educational subjects required for Fellowship within the UUA, including, but not limited to, congregational polity, liberal religious education, and UU history. Such advocacy can only improve the quality of education our ministry candidates receive, which will help strengthen our movement.

Ordination

Ordination is not merely a tertiary level of accreditation after graduation and Fellowship, but a mutual commitment to service and support, a calling out of the congregation to service of that community and the world beyond. It is a recognition and affirmation of the skills, talents, and calling of a person to the professional ministry. As one of the highest honors a congregation can grant to an individual, ordination must be reclaimed as a central event in the life of a congregation. We affirm the recommendations for all clergy from the 1992 report of the Commission on Appraisal:[7]

Ordination is more than just a recognition of service well done; it is the commitment of the community and the ordained minister to continue the work of the church in the world.

- That an educational process be initiated to promote a clearer understanding of ordination within our movement, with congregations encouraged to reclaim their central role.
- That ordination should be in relationship with a congregation the minister presently serves, or will continue to serve in some capacity.
- That ordination signify a calling to service yet to come, not a reward for service rendered.
- That in general only those in Fellowship with the UUA be ordained.[8]

An educational process is necessary for congregations to understand the centrality of their role and the responsibility they are granted by the right to ordain. Most congregations do not consider the appropriate criteria for ordination before an individual asks to be ordained. Yet this is one of the most important decisions a congregation can be asked to make, for ordination is for the life of the clergyperson, unlike the granting of Ministerial Fellowship (recognition of proper credentials, ability, and calling), which can be removed if the individual does not live up to expected standards. Few congregations regret their decision to ordain, but by working with a clear vision and predetermined criteria, we can reduce even those few instances.

Ordination ought ideally to be offered to a person who will have a continuing relationship with the congregation. At its heart, ordination is more than just a recognition of service well done; it is the commitment of the community and the ordained minister to continue the work of the church in the world. Because few congregations are in a position to determine suitability for ministry, we affirm our earlier recommendation that except in special circumstances, only people in Fellowship with the Association be offered ordination by a congregation.

This is a delicate issue, because the right to ordain is held unconditionally by congregations. And yet our partnership in governing means we must rely upon each other's judgment in decision making. Just as congregations should be more active in the recruitment and formation of ministers, congregations should also take serious note when the Fellowship Committee decides not to extend Fellowship to particular individuals.

Before offering the rite of ordination to anyone, particularly someone not in Fellowship, the congregation should establish a careful screening process that takes into account the reservations conveyed by the Fellowship Committee. Such criteria should be stated in writing and congregations should consider reflecting the salient points in their governing documents. As well, we would hope that congregants have had an ongoing relationship with the person they are seeking to ordain and have been able to observe the person's ministry over time.[9]

If after such a review the congregation decides to ordain an individual not in Fellowship, we recommend that such ordination should be clearly understood and stated as ordination to the ministry of *that particular congregation*, not to the Unitarian Universalist ministry as a whole. If the person is later received into Fellowship with the UUA, an ordination certificate would be issued by the Department of Ministry recognizing that person as ordained to our movement. This recommendation would hold true for all clergy not in Fellowship, regardless of whether they are serving in a parish, religious education, or community ministry. We urge the UUA Department of Ministry to develop certificates recognizing ordination by a congregation into its ministry.

For ministers in Fellowship who are serving the wider community, we recommend that the ordaining body should be the congregation or congregations that will serve as the covenanting congregation(s) of the community minister.[10] Ordination of community ministers may also include representatives from the site where the minister will carry out her or his ministry.

The ordination should also include acceptance by the ordinand of her or his responsibility to the community of autonomous congregations, the movement as a whole, and the larger community outside the walls of the congregation. This is not meant as a "loyalty oath," but as a recognition of the interdependence and interrelatedness of all our clergy and congregations. As well, few clergy serve only one congregation or agency during their professional careers; vows to the community of autonomous congregations (the Association) would acknowledge this fact.

Community Ministry

Ministry is the central, defining function of the dedicated religious community. This ministry is directed both inward to its own membership and outward to the world. One of the earliest examples of ministry to the community is that of the Benevolent Fraternity of Unitarian Churches (UU Urban Ministry). Established in Boston in the late 1800s, its founder, Joseph Tuckerman, convinced the congregations that their responsibilities did not end at the church door—their mission was to the world as well as to those within their walls. Tuckerman and his successors in the Benevolent Fraternity did not separate their ministry in the city from their ministry to the gathered community and found their accountability to be both to congregation and community.

In succeeding generations, community ministry took various forms in both Unitarianism and Universalism. Throughout our history, laypeople and clergy have been actively involved in most of the social service and human justice issues in Canada and the United States. We have been active in almost every struggle for human rights, from voting rights, to access to better education, housing, and medical care, to ending various forms of discrimination. A key part of our understanding of ourselves—theologically and humanistically—is that we are and should be active in the greater world outside the walls of our congregations. Our ministry extends into the community at large, whether organized through congregational projects or the individual labor of members.

Our commitment to service to the world extends to our congregations as well as to our clergy. We recommend that congregations continue to find ways of supporting and fostering ministry to the world beyond their doors. Service can include work on a wide variety of social justice projects or sponsorship of the work of a community-based minister. If we believe in the community of autonomous congregations, we must also realize that our religious movement calls us to see that community as having responsibilities to the greater community.

Community Ministry and Congregational Polity

To fully implement our ministry to the world, we need to understand how such community ministry is structurally related to our governance system. Since its official recognition as a separate category of ministry in 1991, community ministry has been seen more as an adjunct than a viable part of our movement. How can our community of autonomous congregations support ordained clergy who go out into the world on our behalf?

The church is in essence the gathered community. Without people coming together—for worship, work, play, education, care, and concern—there would be no Unitarian Universalism. Instead, there would be a collection of people scattered throughout the country who hold similar beliefs, but are not a church, a gathered community. We exist by the fact that we come together.

As we come together, we also profess the belief that the "ministry" of the church is not just that performed by our called professional religious leaders, but belongs to the gathered community. *Ministry is the work of everyone within the congregation and everyone is accountable to the whole for the ministry they undertake.*

Under congregational polity, ordained clergy serving in parishes—whether ministers of religious education or parish ministers—are accountable directly to congregations in several ways that laypeople are not. Three obvious ways are through the right of congregations to call and dismiss clergy; the payment through budgetary approval of salary, housing, and benefits; and the periodic reaffirmation of the ministry through direct evaluation. This accountability extends to their ministry beyond the larger community. Ministers become Unitarian Universalist ministers through their involvement in our congregations.

Likewise, community-based ministers also become (and remain) Unitarian Universalist ministers (rather than ministers called by "the holy spirit," "the Pope," the "holy," the "divine," or a personal sense of call and vocation) through their involvement with the community. To be defined as a Unitarian Universalist minister requires the ordination of a UU congregation.[11] Since the congregation is the basic unit of our governance system, to retain a more authentic Unitarian Universalist identity, ordained community-based ministers should also retain an active involvement within the "community of autonomous congregations."

A Three-way Covenantal Association

Therefore, we recommend that each community minister enter into a three-way covenantal association among (1) the minister, (2) the settings of ministry, and (3) at least one nearby Unitarian Universalist congregation. This recommendation applies to all those in Fellowship as community ministers as well as those in Fellowship in another category but serving outside a parish setting (for example, ministers serving as theological school faculty, military chaplains, or at the UUA or other affiliated organizations). This requirement is comparable to the accountability of parish-based clergy to the congregations they serve.

In the covenantal association, the minister would be accountable to the setting of ministry to fulfill its agenda and the congregation would need to extend its understanding of the ministry to the agency and the minister involved. The community minister would help the congregation understand its role in the wider community and the congregation would help to anchor the minister within a community of hope and justice, providing support and nurturance in the minister's work on behalf of the entire community. The community minister would be accountable to the congregation for the integrity of her or his work in the setting of ministry.

We suggest that the community minister's involvement with the congregation occasionally include, but not be limited to, leading worship, teaching, maintaining collegial relationships with the congregation's parish-based ministers, and reporting on ministerial work outside the congregation. It is assumed that the congregation would offer financial compensation to the community minister for services rendered directly to the congregation.

Covenantal association would remind the community-based minister that one source of power and authority to minister comes from our congregations—the gathered community. Covenantal association would also affirm the role of the community minister within our "community of autonomous

To strengthen our religious leadership, many changes need to be instituted in both our thought processes and systems.

congregations" and would strengthen the congregation's understanding that the ministry of the church must extend beyond the walls of the building. Covenantal association would remind the people in the setting of ministry that the minister is accountable within a larger context, and that he or she is viewed as a valuable and viable member of a larger religious community.

We also believe that inherent in our understanding of the community of autonomous congregations is the responsibility for congregations to seek out and support viable community ministries within their areas. There is much to be gained by participation with community ministry programs, and we recommend that congregations look for ways in which they can enhance their ministry to the wider world by becoming involved in covenantal associations with community ministers.

To this end, the covenanting congregation or congregations should be in geographical proximity to the site of the community ministry, that is, close enough that the congregation(s) can have a clear sense of the work undertaken by the community minister and can recognize their connection with the program. The covenant could be entered into by one or several congregations—the most logical choices are area clusters or districts. We believe that it would be inappropriate for the UUA to be the covenanting congregation since the Association as a whole cannot be actively involved in supporting, evaluating, and collaborating with community ministers. However, we recognize that the UUA would be involved in covenantal associations as the site of ministry for ministers working for the UUA.

We recommend that the ordaining congregation(s) for new community ministers should be the congregation(s) involved in the three-way covenantal association, subject to the other recommendations set out above. For community ministers, covenanting congregations are the closest equivalent to the "calling congregation" for those entering into parish-based ministry.

Relationships to the UUA

Once a community minister is in covenantal association with a congregation, we recommend that the minister be considered settled and thereby eligible for automatic voting privileges at General Assembly. We urge the UUA to investigate whether such covenantal association would entitle community ministers to UUA health care and retirement plans. The Department of Ministry can help to create models of covenantal association for linking community ministers and congregations.

Community-based ministers should not expect to receive the same type of settlement services from the Department of Ministry as parish-based clergy. The nature of community ministry is so diverse and the possible settings for such ministry so numerous that the current and anticipated resources in the department cannot adequately support settlement assistance. However, we recommend that the Department of Ministry continue to provide career guidance and advice, maintain and disseminate information on placement and professional organizations available to community ministers, publicize any specifically Unitarian Universalist community ministry possibilities, and explore ways to make such assistance readily available to community ministers.

Further, we recommend that chapters of the Unitarian Universalist Ministers Association take community-based ministers into account when planning their programs. Care should be taken to ensure that not all programming is designed for or accessible only to those in parish-based ministry settings.

Summary

To strengthen our religious leadership, many changes need to be instituted in both our thought processes and systems. We need to embrace the understanding that as a "community of autonomous congregations" we are deeply connected through all levels of religious leadership and cannot work or live in isolation. Our future existence may not depend on learning to operate as a community of autonomous congregations; unless we apply this belief to our structures of religious leadership, we will be diminished.

Recommendations

1. The categories of parish, religious education, and community ministry should be abolished and individuals should be received into Fellowship as ministers, with the potential for adding areas of specialization.

2. The areas of ministerial specialization should be defined by the Ministerial Fellowship Committee, which would establish requirements for experience and education for these areas.

3. All clergy, regardless of where they serve, should be active members of a Unitarian Universalist congregation.

4. Through districts or other area groupings, congregations should enter into wide-ranging conversations about common goals that should underpin lay ministry.

5. We affirm the Commission on Appraisal's 1992 recommendation that

congregations and the Association work together in the recruitment of individuals for ministry and the formation of those individuals.

6. The Department of Ministry should formulate standards and guidelines that congregations can use in making decisions about sponsoring individuals for the UU ministry.

7. Congregations should review and adopt the criteria for sponsorship well before any person comes to them requesting sponsorship.

8. The needs of Meadville/Lombard Theological School and Starr King School for the Ministry, schools that support the UU movement, should continue to be given priority in funding decisions by the Panel on Theological Education.

9. The Panel on Theological Education should continue to advocate at non-Unitarian Universalist theological schools to encourage the schools to offer students the broad range of educational subjects required for Fellowship within the UUA, including, but not necessarily limited to, congregational polity, liberal religious education, and UU history.

10. We affirm the recommendations for all clergy in the Commission on Appraisal's 1992 report:

    - That an educational process be initiated to promote a clearer understanding of ordination within our movement, with congregations encouraged to reclaim their central role
    - That ordination should be in relationship with a congregation the minister presently serves or will continue to serve in some capacity
    - That ordination signify a calling to service yet to come, not a reward for service rendered
    - That in general only those in Fellowship with the UUA be ordained.

11. Ordination of a person not in Fellowship should be clearly understood and stated as ordination to the ministry of *that particular congregation*, not to the Unitarian Universalist ministry as a whole.

12. The UUA Department of Ministry should develop certificates recognizing ordination by a congregation into its ministry of individuals not in Fellowship with the UUA.

13. The ordaining body should ideally be the congregation(s) with which the professional minister will have an ongoing relationship. For min-

isters in Fellowship serving the wider community, we recommend that the ordaining body be the congregation or congregations that will serve as the covenanting congregation(s) of the community minister.

14. Ordination should include acceptance by the ordinand of responsibility to the community of autonomous congregations, the movement as a whole, and the larger community outside the walls of the congregation.

15. The *Ordination Handbook* prepared by the Department of Ministry should be revised to include the recommendations in this report.

16. Congregations should find ways of supporting and fostering ministry to the world beyond their doors.

17. Community ministers should enter into a three-way covenantal association among the minister, the setting(s) in which they carry out their ministry, and at least one nearby Unitarian Universalist congregation.

18. Congregations should look for ways to enhance their ministry to the wider world by becoming involved in covenantal associations with community-based ministers.

19. The covenanting congregation or congregations should be in geographical proximity to the site of the community ministry.

20. As long as a community minister is in covenantal association with a congregation, the minister should be considered settled and thereby eligible for automatic voting privileges at General Assembly.

21. The Department of Ministry should help to create models of covenantal association for linking community ministers and congregations.

22. The Department of Ministry should continue to provide career guidance and advice, maintain and disseminate information on placement and professional organizations available to community ministers, publicize specifically Unitarian Universalist community ministry possibilities, and explore ways to make this assistance readily available to community ministers.

23. Chapters of the Unitarian Universalist Ministers Association should take community-based ministers into account when planning their programs, both as to meeting times and meeting content.

Sources

Conversations with Stephen Shick, Unitarian Universalist Service Committee; Barbara Jo Sorensen, chair, Society for the Larger Ministry; Diane Miller, director of the Department of Ministry; Ellen Brandenburg, director of ministerial education; Daniel Hotchkiss, settlement director; Rebecca Parker, president, Starr King School for the Ministry; Patti Lawrence, dean of students and congregational life, Starr King School for the Ministry; Neil Shadle, associate professor of ministry and director of field education, Meadville/Lombard Theological School; Ian Evison, interim academic dean and assistant professor of practical theology, Meadville/Lombard Theological School; and Judy Mannheim, associate dean, Modified Residency Program and Continuing Education, and instructor in religious education, Meadville/Lombard Theological School; and the 1993 UUA Women and Religion Survey.

Notes

1. For more information on perceptions about ministers of religious education, see Section 11, "Marginalized Groups."
2. Commission on Appraisal, *Our Professional Ministry: Structure, Support and Renewal* (Boston: Unitarian Universalist Association, 1992), p. 5.
3. Barbara Child, ed., *The Shared Ministry Sourcebook: Resources for Clergy and Laity Ministering Together in Unitarian Universalist Churches* (Boston: Unitarian Universalist Association, 1996), based on the results of the 1993 UUA Women and Religion Committee survey.
4. Barbara Child, "Lay Leaders and Ministers as Partners: New Ways of Doing Ministry," in *The Communicator*, Unitarian Universalist Women's Federation Newsletter, September/October 1993, pp. 1, 4.
5. *Our Professional Ministry*, pp. 8-9, 94.
6. Another possible model is that of the "Consultation on Ministry," whereby candidates for ministry are involved in a weekend retreat sponsored by the Department of Ministry and the Ministerial Fellowship Committee. Details of this type of retreat are set out in Appendix A to the Commission on Appraisal's 1992 report, *Our Professional Ministry: Structure, Support and Renewal*.
7. Details of our recommendations regarding ordination of community ministers can be found further on in this section.
8. *Our Professional Ministry*, p. 62.
9. Programs like those outlined in the previous section (retreats of laypeople, candidates for ministry, and ordained clergy) could be of invaluable assistance in this determination process.

10. Covenanting congregations are those that enter into a three-way relationship among (1) the community-based minister, (2) the site where the minister carries out her or his duties, and (3) the congregation that affirms this as part of its ministry. Details of this structure and our recommendations about it are set out in more detail further on in this section.
11. The exception is ministers ordained in another tradition who are subsequently received into Fellowship as transfer candidates. A second ordination service would not be required in addition to MFC approval.

SECTION TEN

Social Justice

Social justice work has long been a part of Unitarian Universalism, and for almost as long it has been a source of tension within and among congregations. One dearly held value—the right to freedom of belief—at times conflicts with our belief that collective social justice work is crucial to who we are as religious people. Congregations need to explore ways of making decisions about social justice actions that affirm both the right to individual belief and the responsibility for corporate social justice action. This section suggests several approaches to decision making about social justice issues.

The following words of James Luther Adams, delivered to Collegium: An Association for Liberal Religious Studies in 1975, point to the theological centrality of social justice to Unitarian Universalism.

> Liberal religion's attitude of mind we generally characterize as a critical stance before mere tradition, impatience with creeds once-for-all delivered, the rejection of coercion in religion, freedom of conscience, open-mindedness, tolerance—the liberation of the human spirit from heteronomous authorities. Beautiful attitudes! But attitudes alone do not make or change history. The road to hell is paved with good attitudes. They require institutional embodiment. Indeed, the liberal attitudes mentioned appeared initially in the seventeenth century in connection with a power struggle undertaken in order to change social structure. This struggle was a revolutionary institutional struggle, a struggle against the cage of centralized power in church and state and economic order.

Our congregations should see social justice as an important part of their corporate ministry to the world.

Congregational polity was the new conception of a covenanted church that gave form to this struggle, a polity separating the church from the state, placing responsibility upon the members (the consent of the governed), and giving rise to a self-governing congregation.[1]

As Adams notes, we are not a religious tradition with a creed, but a religious movement that has always wedded social justice work to theology. Before their merger, Unitarians and Universalists were active in making the world a better place, through involvement in abolition, women's suffrage, temperance, prison reform, and numerous other causes that sought to improve the human condition. After merger, activism continued in the areas of civil rights, the peace movement, the feminist movement, gay and lesbian liberation, and the ecological movement—to name a few. Many of our congregations offered sanctuary to draft resisters, provided staging areas for local civil rights marches, organized buses to demonstrations across the United States, worked for the Equal Rights Amendment to the United States Constitution, provided sanctuary to "aliens," both in Canada and the United States, and began recycling programs in their communities. Many people came to UU congregations first and foremost because of our liberal voice in the community on these important issues.

The Importance of Social Justice Work

In fact, many of our fastest-growing congregations can point to their involvement in social justice issues as a catalyst to their vitality and growth. The congregation in Portland, Oregon, grew tremendously following its public statements against the proposition to deny gay and lesbian people their human rights. Attendance and membership at our rural church in Ruthven, Ontario (outside Windsor), swelled after an article in the local newspaper detailed the minister's exclusion from the local clergy association because she was not a Christian. Both congregations made clear through their social justice stances that they were religious homes where all were welcome, regardless of society's perceptions. Countless other examples exist—from study of issues to direct service, to advocacy and witness work, and to community organizing—in every community where there are Unitarian Universalists. Scratch a social justice issue and you'll find one of our followers.

It cannot be emphasized enough that Unitarian Universalism entails not only the right and responsibility to come to our own theological understanding—a freedom of belief—but that freedom of belief also calls us, demands us, to participate in social justice work. In the words of James Luther Adams, "Right attitudes are never sufficient alone. They must find embodiment in social institutions. Indeed, one must say that one does not even understand the meaning of 'right attitudes' or even of a theology until one recognizes their implications for social organization."[2] The "rightness" of our theological beliefs cannot be understood without our involvement in trying to make the world reflect the values we hold. For that reason, social justice, and in particular collective social justice, are required for a full understanding of Unitarian Universalism.

At this point we run into the complexities of congregational polity, in the wide diversity in how congregations approach social justice work. Some empower a social justice or social responsibility committee to be active on behalf of and in the name of the congregation, or only in the name of the committee, or only as individuals. Others allow such committees to work and exist, but not to invoke the name of the congregation. Some congregations have a series of task forces that look at specific issues or programs. Others earmark a certain percentage of their budget or pledges, or raise funds to support the social justice outreach programs of the congregation. Some governing boards are allowed to make statements on behalf of the congregation, whereas others are not. Some congregations require a simple majority of the congregation, whereas others require a super-majority, or never take action as a congregation.

As well, the understanding of what constitutes social justice work varies widely. A vast continuum of actions is designated as social justice work: educating oneself and the community, signing petitions, working hands-on in the community, sponsoring events, collecting and donating money, protesting, marching, undertaking civil disobedience, writing letters to the media—all these and more are aspects of social justice, but may not be recognized as such within individual congregations.[3] There is an almost infinite number of ways that we understand and place "the responsibility upon the members (the consent of the governed)," to quote Adams. Social justice work within Unitarian Universalist congregations is deeply related to our response to marginalized groups, both within our congregations and society at large. See also "Marginalized Groups," Section 11 of this report.

Congregational Fears

Collective congregational social justice is central and crucial to living out what it means to be Unitarian Universalist. Our congregations should see social justice as an important part of their corporate ministry—their service—to the world. Accordingly, a good social justice program should enjoy broad support and involvement in the congregation. We recognize that there are valid concerns about the unintended repercussions of such con-

We must not let our fear of division be the determining factor in social justice work.

gregational activity, but believe it better to err on the side of action rather than inaction.

Many fears arise about the inadvertent effects of corporate social justice work. Some members dislike congregational social justice action for fear of divisions or conflicts that will arise in the decision-making process. This fear is not unfounded: Our congregations have divided over social justice issues from the involvement of the United States in the world wars, through the US involvement in the Vietnam War, the Civil Rights movement, the pro-choice movement, and gay and lesbian liberation. Conflicts over war-related issues affect not only US congregations; several Canadian congregations actively worked against World War II and especially on behalf of draft dodgers during the Vietnam era—not always to universal approval.

Yet we must not let our fear of division be the determining factor in social justice work. To quote William Gardiner, director of Faith in Action: A UUA Department for Diversity and Justice,

> Conflict doesn't only happen around social justice issues in the congregation. Many (some would say all) decisions in the life of the church involve conflict. Questions arise: Should we build a new organ or keep the old one? What kind of hymns should we sing? What kind of music should we have on Sunday morning? Should the minister wear a robe or not? Sometimes people can get very heated about these issues. It is unfair to single out social justice as being especially conflict laden.... The congregation needs to address how it processes controversy in any area of its life."[4]

Sometimes our ideas about social justice decision-making processes become coupled with an erroneous understanding of congregational polity applied to the individual member. People reason that if no congregation can be told what to do by any other congregation, then no member of a congregation can be told what to believe or do as far as social justice and social witness are concerned. In an apparent attempt to honor the diversity within our movement, some people take our theological process and this limited understanding of congregational polity to mean that no congregation can speak out on social justice issues without the consent of the entire congregation. Instead, the congregation defines its role as supporting its members in their individual contributions to the social justice realm.

The Need for Social Justice Involvement

These are persuasive arguments against carrying out social justice work in our congregations. However, when our congregations cannot speak individually or collectively, we all lose a broader voice within the community. In contrast to other religions that do speak out and speak out forcefully on issues, we give up the ability to have a voice that is greater than that of the individual, and we lose the chance to demonstrate that there is a vital liberal religious movement working on many important social justice issues. As William Gardiner writes, "The principle of freedom of conscience does not exist by itself. It exists in relation to other important principles of our faith like the responsibility to seek the truth and the commitment to act on those beliefs which are passionately held. A vital liberal faith will find a creative balance between these three important principles."[5]

When our congregations cannot speak individually or collectively, we all lose a broader voice within the community.

Another reason that social justice work may be fraught with conflict is that often social justice is envisioned in one way—marching and demonstrating with signs and banners proclaiming a congregation's position on a particular issue. But this image is a small picture of social justice potential. As stated earlier, social justice may include education, service, advocacy, witnessing, and community organizing. It can include education for the congregation or the community at large on a variety of issues, from the controversial (abortion, assisted suicide, gun control, and the death penalty) to the non-controversial (prenatal care, information on choosing nursing homes for aged or ill family members, and grief recovery).

Service can include cleaning up trash alongside a highway, providing religious services for correctional institutions, serving food to the homeless, or shoveling snow for shut-ins. Advocacy could mean helping those labelled mentally ill to find access to diminishing services, or filing tax returns for the elderly. Witnessing could be standing silently by at funerals for young people killed by violence, attending rallies led by Mothers Against Drunk Driving, or undertaking civil disobedience outside a nuclear power plant. Community organizing could be working with Habitat for Humanity to build a new home in the neighborhood or fighting city hall to get public housing projects upgraded and made safer. There is a wide gamut of potential ways of being socially active and every congregation within the UUA should be able to find a unifying way to engage their beliefs for the improvement of its community.

We must also remember that to decide not to decide or act is in itself a decision on social justice work within the congregation. William Gardiner states:

> Finally, the idea that the church should take no position on moral issues seems to be self-contradictory—for taking no action is in itself a form

[of] action. This was clearly shown in the case of the German churches that did not speak out against Hitler as he rose to power. This unwillingness to speak out led to terrible consequences for millions of people across the world. The result of not taking a position on issues is to support the status quo. Not to decide is to decide.[6]

Social Justice Decision Making

Taking no action is in itself a form [of] action.

Congregational polity calls us not only to be active in the world, but to be active in a way that honors the diversity in our congregations. We recommend that whatever process congregations use to determine their social justice work be a just process that respects the diversity of opinion in the congregation. Making decisions about social justice work in a manner that does not respect the disparate views in our congregations is not a good model. A respectful process involves as many people as possible in the decision-making process, and provides ample time for people to digest issues before determining which action is appropriate. To retain a sense of congregational involvement, action may need to take a less "radical" issue or style of social justice than some might desire.

The Department of Faith in Action has designed a grid for congregations to use in making these key decisions. The grid can be found in William Gardiner's paper, "Congregational Decision Making About Controversial Social Justice Issues," which is available through the Department of Faith in Action.

The Commission also recommends that the process used for making decisions about social justice action include the greatest number of people possible with ample opportunities for education and discussion. Town hall meetings and other vehicles for information and opinion sharing without voting are one option, as are small discussion groups. Care must be taken not to make a decision so quickly that members of the congregation do not feel heard. If the process allows time for deliberation and discussion, then a level of trust can be maintained so that people feel honored in their agreement or disagreement with the majority. We recommend the use of a super-majority—two-thirds or three-quarters of those present, for example—to reduce the possibility of congregations dividing over social justice issues.

We also believe that after due consideration and a vote in accordance with the congregation's decision-making process, people should accept the right of the majority (or super-majority) to act, even if they do not agree personally. Part of being in a democratic community is learning the art of compromise and consensus making, not in the sense that we must all agree, but that we can all go along with the process and the decisions that arise from that process. The *Social Justice Empowerment Program Handbook* created by the Department of Faith in Action provides a resource for congregations working toward framing their social justice agenda. (See Section 6, "Congregational Governance," for a more detailed discussion of the decision-making process.)

It may be, as well, that the best decision on some issues is to refrain from acting, particularly in emergency situations when there is not ample time for information gathering and discussion, or after prolonged debate when no clear consensus emerges. Rather than jeopardize the congregation in these situations, it is better to refrain from acting. However, we hope that the work the congregations do in setting a tenor of social justice action as the norm will greatly limit the frequency of these situations.

On an associational level, the Canadian Unitarian Council has developed a social justice alternative to the UUA Resolution process. When the Canadian Unitarian Council reviewed its social justice stands on several issues, they found that they were often constrained by the particular language of a resolution passed at their Annual General Meeting. To avoid such limitations and to receive input on an issue, one congregation developed a curriculum on death and dying and the social justice issues implied therein. Members of most Canadian congregations took part in the curriculum and then answered open-ended questions about a range of issues covered in the program. The Canadian Unitarian Council (CUC) reviewed the completed questionnaires and prepared a consensus statement on the various issues. Rather than creating resolutions about specific situations or conditions, the CUC has data available on many aspects of death and dying so that the board can respond to a variety of situations with valid input from its constituencies.

Similarly, individual congregations could entertain views on a variety of issues, complete questionnaires, and using majority-supermajority rules, empower a committee or board to speak on behalf of the congregation on the basis of the information contained in the questionnaires.

In some congregations and some districts or larger groupings of congregations, movement toward collective social justice programming will be more difficult than in others. Where the ethic of individual rights and freedoms is accentuated to a greater degree than the responsibility to the collective, it may be more difficult for individuals to give up their autonomy for the greater whole. However, if we are to reach our potential as a religious movement and if we are to fully embrace the concept of the "community of autonomous congregations," we need to be willing to recognize and emphasize our interrelatedness.

Social Justice Work on the Associational Level

While we encourage congregations to increase their social justice involvement, we also uphold the right and need for the Unitarian Universalist Association as a whole to remain actively engaged in social justice work. This is a complex issue for our multinational Association. Social justice issues vary greatly between nations and the approaches taken must be specific to the culture in which the issues arise. For example, the nature of racism in the United States is different than in Canada, and issues about racism are different in Canada than in Australia, New Zealand, the Philippines, and the other nations in which UUA member congregations are found. The UUA Board and staff do not have the knowledge or expertise to address social justice issues in all nations. For Canadian Unitarian Universalists, collective national social justice work can be carried out by the Canadian Unitarian Council. In the United States, the answer is not as clear because of the multinational nature of the UUA.

Although we recognize the complexity of the issue, we still hold that collective social justice is a priority for our religious movement. Therefore, we recommend that the UUA Board of Trustees continue to be empowered to make statements on behalf of the Association on social justice issues within the United States, especially in cases where General Resolutions already exist. In addition, we recommend that the Board continue to work for social justice by supporting the Department of Faith in Action's submission of *amici curi* legal briefs and engaging in collaborative work with interfaith coalitions on key issues. Working on social justice issues is a key part of who we are as a religious people. To ensure that we remain consistent with our principles, the UUA Board must be empowered to act on social justice issues as it sees fit, bearing in mind the diversity of the Association. This diversity is also the reason that we suggest that the UUA Board's statements be limited to social justice issues in the United States.

We also recommend that congregations become (or remain) active in the resolutions process through engagement with the study resolutions and action on resolutions adopted by General Assembly. Congregations may also submit comments, suggestions, and amendments to resolutions without having to attend General Assembly. We also encourage increased congregational involvement in General Assembly, not only on social justice issues but also to further our connections as "a community of autonomous congregations." (See Section 7, "Cooperative Relationships," for more discussion on issues related to the resolutions process and suggestions for increasing participation at General Assembly.)

Summary

We affirm our belief that collective social justice activity is an integral part of Unitarian Universalism and necessary for living out our theological approach. Such action should be retained and strengthened, using decision-making processes that are just and respectful of diversity of opinion. Action for social justice in no way violates congregational polity, but rather provides a way for understanding the increased power of working together as a "community of autonomous congregations."

Recommendations

1. The process that congregations use to determine social justice work should be just and respectful of the diversity of opinion in the congregation.

2. The process used for making decisions about social justice action should include the greatest number of people possible with ample opportunity for education and discussion.

3. A super-majority—two-thirds or three-quarters of those present, for example—should be used to reduce the possibility of congregations dividing over social justice issues.

4. The UUA Board of Trustees should continue to be empowered to make statements on behalf of the Association on social justice issues within the United States, especially in cases where General Resolutions exist. In addition, we recommend that the Board continue to work actively for social justice by supporting the department of Faith in Action's submission of *amici curi* legal briefs and engaging in collaborative work with interfaith coalitions on key issues.

5. Congregations should become (or remain) active in the UUA resolutions process through engagement with the study resolutions and action on resolutions adopted by General Assembly.

Sources

Research was based on the personal experience of the Commissioners; conversations with William Gardiner, director, Faith in Action: A UUA Department for Diversity and Justice; Marilyn Sewell, minister, First Unitarian Church of Portland, Oregon; Anne Treadwell, minister, Unitarian Universalist Church of Olinda, Ruthven, Ontario; written materials from Faith in Action, particularly "Congregational Decision Making About Controversial Social Justice Issues" by William Gardiner and the *Social Justice Empowerment Program Handbook.*

Notes

1. James Luther Adams, "From Cage to Covenant," in *The Prophethood of All Believers*, edited by George K. Beach (Boston: Beacon Press, 1986), p. 136.
2. James Luther Adams, "Theological Bases of Social Action," in *On Being Human Religiously*, edited by Max L. Stackhouse (Boston: Unitarian Universalist Association, 1976), p. 114.
3. Details on the continuum of social justice work appear in several publications published by the Department of Faith in Action, as well as in *Our Chosen Faith: An Introduction to Unitarian Universalism* by John Buehrens and F. Forrester Church (Boston: Beacon Press, 1989).
4. William Gardiner, "Congregational Decision Making About Controversial Social Justice Issues," January 12, 1996, p. 12. (Paper available through Faith in Action.)
5. *Ibid.*, p. 3.
6. *Ibid.*, p. 5.

SECTION ELEVEN

Marginalized Groups

How power is used in negotiating difference is among the most difficult of all issues faced by institutions—particularly those that choose to be in voluntary association such as religious institutions. In fact, the major pressure points of conflict in our understandings of congregational polity revolve around the dilemma of power and difference. This section explores how prevailing understandings of congregational polity may enhance or inhibit our well-being as an association of congregations living with the reality of differences in power and identity in our multitheological and increasingly multicultural religious movement.

Like most groups, Unitarian Universalists define themselves in terms of demographics, values, lifestyle, associations, modes of behavior, social, and theological orientation. These factors, which exist at the center of our movement and characterize our dominant cultural ethos and identity, are what sociologist Robert Bellah refers to as a group's "habits of association."

We might better understand Unitarian Universalism as a social system if we consider not only the characteristics, values, and patterns that are normative for those at the center of our movement, but the characteristics of those at the margins—those who do not fit the Unitarian Universalist norm.

William Connolly has explored group identity in relation to difference. Just as heresy is defined in relation to orthodoxy, identity (both individual and social) is defined in relation to other identities.[1] Similarly, marginality exists only in relation to centrality. Theologian Jung Young Lee reminds us that "marginality and centrality are so mutually inclusive and relative that it is imbalanced to stress one more than the other."[2] In other

What is normative for mainstream Unitarian Universalists is not necessarily normative for those at the margins of our movement.

words, centrality can be defined only in relation to marginality and vice versa. Thus who we *are not* helps to inform who we *are* as a religious movement. The "habits of association" of both groups are context-based, determined by the history, background, and social location of the group's members.

Although there are clear signs of preparation for change—if not social transformation in the Unitarian Universalist movement—with the notable exception of women gaining acceptance as ministers and leaders, the UU movement is still largely influenced by its pre-1970s identity as a liberal religious movement whose members are primarily of European American heritage, highly educated, heterosexual, "come-outers" with a humanist/existentialist bent.[3] See Section 5, "The Spiritual and Cultural Ethos of Unitarian Universalism," for a fuller exploration of this topic.

The "Non-discrimination" Clause: Bylaw Ambiguity

Article II, Section C-2.3, of the UUA Bylaws is the most frequently cited reference that guides our decision making and action about open membership and non-discrimination. Accordingly:

> the Association declares and affirms its special responsibility, and that of its member societies and organizations, to promote the full participation of persons in all of its and their activities and in the full range of human endeavor without regard to race, color, sex, disability, affectional or sexual orientation, age or national origin and without requiring adherence to any particular interpretation of religion or to any particular religious belief or creed.

It is this statement that many people understand as a non-discrimination clause with particular application to numerical minority and marginalized groups. A pressure point that bears on congregational polity is that there is no common understanding of the meaning of "non-discrimination" or "open membership" based on Article II, Section C-2.3. This bylaw is highly ambiguous because the assumptions are not stated and there is no agreement among Unitarian Universalists about the following questions:

- Are Unitarian Universalist congregations open (or should they be) to anyone who wishes to join, including those who promote hatred against a particular group? Should a membership standard be applied that is consistent with the UUA Bylaws, especially the Principles and Purposes? Is applying such a standard authoritative, a creed in disguise, coercive, or discriminatory?

- Are intentional congregations (those designed to meet group-specific needs) inherently good or are they discriminatory?
- Are individuals or congregations obliged to adhere to the Principles and Purposes, including the imposition of any standard of membership?

One interpretation of Article II, Section C-2.3, focuses on a section of the language of the bylaw: "to promote the *full participation* of persons in all of its and their activities and in the full range of human endeavor *without regard to* race, color. . . ." This clause has been interpreted to mean that our congregations and the activities of the Association should serve *all* people who wish to be included. In this scenario, "*without regard to . . .*" assumes that difference (based on race, gender, sexual orientation, physical ability, or theology, for example) need not be a special consideration. Further, it is assumed that an ideal group is a group in which differences are not emphasized, that assimilation into the mainstream is desirable. The logical conclusion of such an argument is that intentional congregations—those designed to meet group-specific needs (e.g., gays and lesbians, Latino/as, humanists)—are exclusive congregations and therefore antithetical to the intent of this bylaw.

A second interpretation of this Article is based on the assumption that authentic diversity is best supported by pluralism, not assimilation; that a pluralistic group is one that intentionally supports and highlights differences as inherently good and encourages each group to express its uniqueness and integrity; that for a group to be true to itself, differences cannot (or should not) be deemphasized through acculturation or assimilation into the mainstream.

A third interpretation focuses on the opening phrase, "the Association declares and affirms its special responsibility . . . to promote the full participation of . . ."; this emphasis supports a pluralistic viewpoint.

These ambiguities and multiple interpretations lead some people to argue that the language of Article II, Section C-2.3, is paradoxical, if not contradictory. In any case, there is no agreement on the question of who is or is not welcome in our congregations. Indeed, this remains a point of conflict that directly affects how congregational polity is understood in our congregations and the Association. For a discussion of other ambiguities in the UUA Bylaws, see Section 4, "The UUA Bylaws: A Study in Ambivalence."

Majority and Minority Norms in Conflict

During the past three decades, we have struggled to address issues that arise out of multiple understandings of the Bylaws and the Principles and Purposes. On the one hand, considerable efforts have been made to better understand and struggle through our differences, to teach not only tolerance but also respect for our diversity and to reaffirm our faith in "the inherent worth and dignity of every person." On the other hand, many of our decisions and practices are based on the assumption that the norms and values held by the majority in an earlier era serve us well today. More important than the recognition of any one group now considered to be marginalized is a larger issue that frequently gets lost: What is normative for mainstream Unitarian Universalists is not necessarily normative for those at the margins of our movement. How one understands this issue in relation to congregational polity has massive implications for the future of our movement—whether we will grow—and if we grow, whether we will duplicate our demographic profile or grow through diversity.

For purposes of this report, marginalized groups in Unitarian Universalism include:

- gay, lesbian, bisexual, or transgender people
- people of color
- the physically and/or mentally challenged
- the working class and those who are not college educated
- young adults (ages 18-35) and youth (ages 14-18).

These groups represent the current focal point of anti-oppression initiatives in the UUA Department of Faith in Action and *Weaving the Fabric of Diversity,* an adult education curriculum produced by the UUA Department of Religious Education. Other marginalized groups within the UU movement include Canadian Unitarian Universalists, Unitarian Universalist Christians, neo-pagans or practitioners of earth-centered religions, and those who live in a culture of ultraconservative Christianity.

A Challenge to the Historic Unitarian Universalist Identity

A prevailing assumption among Unitarian Universalists is that marginalized groups should or will be integrated or assimilated into the mainstream.

Between the 1960s and the 1980s, two groups—African Americans and Canadians—compelled Unitarian Universalists to reconsider their identity as an Association, as congregations, and as individuals. In separate venues, both groups captured the attention of the General Assembly, the UUA Board of Trustees and staff by challenging long-held assumptions about Unitarian Universalist values, theological premises, and rules of governance.

While issues of representation and empowerment sparked considerable controversy over the years, an underlying issue was the assumption that Unitarian Universalism would appeal primarily to those who fell within the UU "demographic norm"—which excluded people of color. It was once considered that a logical pathway to growth was to develop marketing strategies to attract people within the existing demographic norm rather than to promote diversity, and a policy recommendation to this effect was made. Fortunately, the UUA did not accept this 1987 recommendation.

There were additional assumptions:

- that Canadian Unitarian Universalists and people of color who were already Unitarian Universalists held values that were consistent with Unitarian Universalist norms
- that people of color and Canadian Unitarian Universalists aspired to mirror the norms and values of (if not to be *like*) Unitarian Universalists in the United States (no doubt presuming a Euro-American ethos)
- that Canadians and people of color could or would easily assimilate or be integrated into the mainstream of Unitarian Universalism.

That women were already a numerical majority (in society at large and within the Unitarian Universalist movement) is central to understanding their empowerment, and it may explain why many non-majority groups in the Association continue to be marginalized. In addition to their lower proportional representation, generally speaking, marginalized groups share the following characteristics:

- They are viewed as unrepresentative of Unitarian Universalism.
- They lack equal access to power and influence in the Association compared with mainstream groups.
- They often feel that they must fight for recognition of their perspectives, interests, and agenda, and for inclusion in our congregations and the Association.

A prevailing assumption among Unitarian Universalists—one that reflects cultural assumptions among the mainstream in the United States—is that marginalized groups should or will be integrated or assimilated into the mainstream. But since the 1960s, US history has shown that this rarely happens. Instead, groups that stand at the margins have challenged dominant group perspectives, norms, values, standards, and assumptions, asserting their own identity, understandings, and interests.

These differing perspectives and competing interests not only challenge our collective identity, but they continue to result in conflict. Congregational polity is often invoked as justification for resisting, if not rejecting, a group that has heretofore been nonexistent or a minority within a local congregation or our movement. In such cases, by sheer numbers the majority tends to prevail—and maintain its power—still believing its position to be fundamentally democratic. But where is the balance between political democracy and theological principles?

Congregational polity is often invoked as justification for rejecting a group that has heretofore been nonexistent or a minority within a local congregation or our movement.

The Canadian Unitarian Council

Canadian and African American expressions of resistance have shown that the assumptions about mainstream assimilation are false. These circumstances lead to an interesting paradox. Until recently, the number of Canadian clergy serving UU congregations on both sides of the border could be counted on two hands. Within the last decade, there has been a great expansion of Canadian clergy and ministerial students; and many more congregations are being led by Canadian-born Unitarians.

At the same time, after the decision to hire a full-time executive director in 1983, the Canadian Unitarian Council (CUC) has become a much more effective and uniquely Canadian voice. The CUC helps congregations deal with social justice, financial, legal, and development issues specific to the Canadian context. Because the criteria for determining the viability of new congregations in the United States are not the same as in Canada, the CUC funds its own extension programs and other programs that do not meet UUA criteria, and cooperates with the UUA on other projects.

Four Marginalized Groups

By the 1980s, women's voices were making their way toward the center of our movement. The gay/lesbian/bisexual/transgender community was gaining power as well. Both groups challenged the assumption that heterosexual and male-centered values, experiences, and aspirations were normative. Today, youth and young adults as well as persons with disabilities have helped us to understand that neither middle age nor being "temporarily able-bodied" represents Unitarian Universalism in its fullness, nor should be considered normative. Though Unitarian Universalists remain *the* most highly educated group among 70 religious movements,[4] because of (at least in part) the new strength of groups previously at the margins of Unitarian Universalism, some of our members have begun to find the courage to acknowledge that they did not attend (or complete) college.

Now we examine four types of marginalization in Unitarian Universalism: the gay, lesbian, bisexual, and transgender community; people of color; children and religious education; and marginalization based on theological views.

1. The Gay, Lesbian, Bisexual, and Transgender Community

The gay, lesbian, bisexual, and transgender community (called LesBiGay) has gained greater acceptance in Unitarian Universalism than in any religious movement (except the Metropolitan Community Church, which was created to meet the needs of this population). While a statistical correlation cannot be made, it is likely that the Welcoming Congregation Program developed by the UUA may account for this acceptance, at least in part. At the same time, this program has created controversy. Although the idea for the program grew out of a 1987 attitudinal survey that documented widespread homophobia and heterosexism among Unitarian Universalists, many congregations already believed that they welcomed all people, including the LesBiGay community.

Citing congregational polity, many congregants expressed displeasure that they would be considered a "welcoming congregation" *only* when certified by the UUA Office of Lesbian, Gay, Bisexual, and Transgender Concerns (OLGBTC). Although such certification is not required but "highly recommended," most congregations that complete the program do, in fact, apply for certification. Based on measurable behavioral objectives, the program suggests steps that aid congregations in moving toward affirming same-sex unions, dedication of the children of same-sex couples, and language that is inclusive of gay, lesbian, bisexual, and transgender relationships. The program also encourages congregations to adopt bylaw changes to include a non-discrimination clause to protect the LesBiGay community from discrimination in hiring or calling a minister. Of course, these behavioral objectives (measurable or not) do not guarantee that a congregation will be free of homophobia and heterosexism.

Certification as a Welcoming Congregation

A pressure point for congregational polity centers around certification as congregations struggle with issues that, to quote Jeanette Hopkins, "by intent or by unawareness, causes or permits gays, lesbians, bisexuals, *et al.* to feel unsafe, unwelcome [or] unaffirmed."[5] The controversy is summed up by a gay man who visited one congregation: "This *feels* like a welcoming congregation to me, but you aren't on the list." Some congregations view the list as a litmus test (which for them seems to be a creedal statement) and have therefore chosen not to participate in the welcoming congregation certification process. Some say that certification sets up a two-tier system and promotes competition, if not a holier-than-thou attitude among congregations.

Though participation is voluntary, critics also say that the welcoming congregation certification process violates congregational polity. In January of 1996, the OLGBTC estimated that only 89 of our 1,039 congregations had been certified.

Hopkins highlights a question that many people have raised: "Why should not Welcoming Congregation certification be awarded also to societies that are racially and economically inclusive (though the suggestion that a society 'welcomes' people of color and the poor seems to have a patronizing

Though participation is voluntary, critics say that the welcoming congregation certification process violates congregational polity.

ring)?" She also asks several critical questions regarding the Welcoming Congregation certification process and congregational polity:

- Will societies that do not apply for certification as Welcoming Congregations be perceived, or even stigmatized, as *un-welcoming*?
- Will people who resist official recognition be seen as homophobic?
- What is the source of an authority to certify?

Many of the issues affecting the LesBiGay community also affect people of color and other marginalized groups who, in contrast to their own self-understandings, have been subjected to the assumptions, beliefs, values, and norms—in short, the dominant paradigm—of Unitarian Universalists.

2. People of Color

A careful review of the UUA Bylaws helps us to understand some of the issues faced by racial or ethnic minorities in Unitarian Universalism. Since the 1961 merger of Unitarianism and Universalism, people of color have been the center of at least three controversies in which congregational polity has been invoked: (1) open membership, (2) the Black Empowerment Controversy, and (3) affirmative action (including the current racial justice and cultural diversity initiative).

Open Membership
One of the issues on the agenda for the 1963 General Assembly was whether to exclude several rural Southern Universalist congregations who, by authority of their bylaws or in practice, excluded African Americans. The proposal to exclude was defeated, based on "the ground that a free religious movement has no power to excommunicate."[6]

The Black Empowerment Era
The years from 1967 to 1982 were a period of stormy relations between Unitarian Universalists of European heritage and those of African heritage. Multiple issues of congregational polity were at the heart of the controversy. Without explicitly naming the controversy as an issue of polity, the 1983 report of the Commission on Appraisal, *Empowerment: One Denomination's Quest for Racial Justice 1967-1982*, gave considerable attention to issues of congregational polity. Readers are encouraged to review that report for background and detail. A brief summary may be helpful in understanding the controversy.

With strong passions and competing ideologies about how racial parity should be approached, self-empowerment strategies of the Black Affairs Council (BAC), the Black Unitarian Universalist Caucus (BUCC), and Black

Who speaks for Unitarian Universalists, anyway? Board of Trustees? General Assembly? Nobody?

and White Alternative (BAWA) flew in the face of existing structures of governance and presumed consensus about how the business of the Association should be carried out. With so many voices claiming power, the matter was further complicated. The controversy called into question notions of Unitarian Universalist identity, structure, and system of governance. To cite the 1983 Commission on Appraisal report, "Who speaks for Unitarian Universalists, anyway? Board of Trustees? General Assembly? Nobody?"[7] The lack of agreement on answers to this question yields a myriad of additional questions about congregational polity:

- What constitutes legitimate authority for a marginalized or disempowered group in the context of a majority group—in this case, Unitarian Universalism—as a voluntary association of autonomous congregations?
- In what ways do the Unitarian Universalist Principles and/or Bylaws call us to enact compensatory or retributive justice for our complicity (direct or indirect) in supporting or maintaining racism and other forms of systemic injustice?
- Given historical injustices and the quest for empowerment of persons of color, should power and authority within the Unitarian Universalist Association be distributed disproportionately to begin to level the playing field?
- Can there be a biracial or multiracial alliance within the UUA in which those who have been historically empowered accept the leadership of those who have been disempowered and oppressed? If so, how should such an alliance be structured?
- To what extent are the General Assembly voting processes and the democratic principles of the Association an effective means to achieving racial justice in the Association?

Since the Empowerment Controversy began more than 20 years ago, we have not had a systematized review of congregational polity or other issues that arose at that time. If we are to learn from the experience, such a review would seem to be a worthwhile endeavor.

The Racial and Cultural Diversity Initiative
Some of the same congregational polity issues that arose in the 1967 to 1982 period are now focused on various aspects of the racial and cultural diversity initiative, which followed the 1992 UUA General Assembly Resolution. It has the following dimensions:

- an affirmative action policy of the UUA Extension Ministry Program (within the Office of Congregational, District, and Extension Services) to offer special support for ministers of color

- special support for intentional congregations—those whose vision is to function in a cultural milieu that is consistent with the racial, ethnic, linguistic, and/or identity needs of people of color.

A number of new and emerging congregations seek to affirm particular racial, ethnic, or cultural groups and to meet the needs of particular communities (e.g., gays and lesbians, Unitarian Universalist Christian congregations, Spanish- or Korean-speaking congregations). Although the Association has established sanctions against congregations that discriminate against individuals on the basis of racial, ethnic, or sexual or affectional orientation, there remains a need for a deeper understanding of intentional congregations whose *raison d'etre* is to express an identity that differs from the Unitarian Universalist norm.

Some Unitarian Universalists believe that intentional congregations (or a special emphasis on any one group within a congregational or associational context) are exclusionary and thus inconsistent with the UUA Bylaws, Article II, Section C-2.3. Deeper discussion is needed about how to balance and negotiate the self-identified *needs* of particular identity groups that have been historically oppressed with the perceived *rights* of groups that have been historically empowered.

Although most people would acknowledge that ministers of color have not begun to approach parity in the Association, achieving parity rests not only on political will or intentionality, but also on how congregational polity is interpreted. Jeanette Hopkins articulates one position: "We have resorted to restrictive *means* to achieve *ends* of openness in efforts to encourage a stronger African-American presence in our churches, in our ministry, and in the Black community."[8]

The central polity issue for marginalized groups is perhaps a question of *means* more than ends. Suspicion of coercion and a belief that the UUA wishes to impose its will on member congregations are among the issues that prevent us from reaching consensus about the means necessary to achieve racial justice as affirmed in the UUA Bylaws (including the Principles and Purposes) and General Assembly resolutions.

3. Children and Religious Education

Religious education is a complex issue. On the one hand, we place high value on religious education for children. On the other hand, how we think about religious educators—both ministers of religious education (MREs) and directors of religious education (DREs)—is sometimes inconsistent with how we think about religious education as a program that is central to faith development. Religious educators have a special identity that is rarely understood or affirmed as a central aspect of congregational life in our movement.

Given that we can point to many vibrant religious education programs throughout our movement, not everyone would agree that children's religious education is, in fact, marginalized. However, if we examine longstanding patterns in religious education, coupled with the self-understanding of those who serve children and families in our congregations, the community of religious educators (MREs and DREs alike) emerges as a marginalized group. As a group, religious educators (both MREs and DREs) have not yet gained equal economic parity or the political clout of those who focus on parish ministry.

Congregational Polity and Religious Education
One of the issues here revolves around congregational polity. Despite the fact that congregational polity requires consensus, decisions about religious education are often made by a relatively small group within a congregation. Religious educators point out that many of those who comprise such committees often do not understand religious education as a ministry to *both* children and families. Nevertheless, they are empowered to determine the foundations of children's religious education, and to make major decisions about programming for children, compensation, visibility, the extent to which religious education is understood within the congregation, and the overall image of what is still largely women's work.

While it should be noted that a small number of men serve our congregations as religious educators, it is not coincidental that the majority are women and that both women and children have been historically marginalized. Women and children are, in fact, the focal point of religious education in most congregations. Reaching parity for MREs is being addressed by the Department of Ministry. Religious education consultants are now available in some districts to address these issues more generally. Our ability to address the issues of congregation-based decision making in relation to the marginalization of women and children depends on our willingness to widen the circle of discussion and decision making in our congregations.

A group of MREs with whom the Commission met pointed to three factors related to "the feminization of religious education." Compared with parish ministers, (1) their work is less valued; (2) their compensation is lower; and (3) MREs, both females and males, are less respected. MREs also pointed to a set of assumptions that affect their professional development and livelihood, including the following:

- MREs are not available for settlement outside their current location
- MREs are not preachers (or there is often surprise that they *can* preach as well as most parish ministers)
- MREs may not work out because (a) they are considered more trouble to congregations than they're worth; (b) they "cost too much"; and (c)

they are generally part of multiple ministry staff teams, which are presumed to be problematic.

Such assumptions tend to spread like wildfire throughout congregations and the Association. Not coincidentally, most such assumptions are posed in direct contrast to parish ministry as normative, which MREs believe leads to the perpetuation of their marginalized status. Directors of religious education cite similar issues as well as the fact that because many are part-time employees, the lack of employee benefits perpetuates their status as second-class workers.

Marginalizing children's religious education in Unitarian Universalism may be related to a discomfort with theology among UU adults. All the evidence points to a general skepticism, if not fear, of serious theological engagement. If parents and adults have not resolved their own theological issues (or if they are unclear about what they believe), it is not surprising that they are uncomfortable with religious education for their children. Although we may be relatively comfortable with the *World Religions* curriculum as a broad approach to religious education, many religious educators told the Commission that one of the questions parents consistently ask is: What are you going to teach my child about the Bible (or about Christianity)? Until we address our personal theological ambiguities, we will unconsciously continue to marginalize children's religious education.

The marginality expressed by ministers of religious education is part of the larger debate throughout the Association about what constitutes ministry. Although we have had three categories of ministry for more than a decade, there is ambiguity (perhaps more among laity than clergy) about the legitimacy of both religious education and community ministry *as ministry*. (See Section 9, "Religious Leadership," for a discussion of community ministry.) Parish ministry is still considered the norm not only in Unitarian Universalism, but in most religious traditions. Many who chose the ministry of religious education or community ministry still feel marginalized within the UU movement. Many issues need to be worked out to make all three categories of ministry not only acceptable, but normative.

Affirmative Action—Yes or No?
The issue of affirmative action and preferences is a controversial one for the LesBiGay community, people of color, and religious educators. The following questions exemplify the nature of the debate:

- Should the Association have affirmative action goals? Should congregations support the Association's efforts to monitor staffing patterns at the UUA with special attention to marginalized groups?
- Should the Association recommend affirmative steps (e.g., the Beyond

Categorical Thinking Program) for congregations perceived as having discriminated against a ministerial candidate based on race, gender, sexual orientation, physical ability, or other reasons?
- Should preferences for job applicants or volunteer positions be stated? For example, in 1992 the Nominating Committee of the Unitarian Universalist Women's Federation (UUWF) announced that candidates "are expected to be committed feminists" and to support "a non-hierarchical work process."[9] Does our system of congregational polity preclude the Association, its member congregations, and associate or affiliate organizations from stating a preference and/or orientation related to commitments, values, beliefs, or organizational processes or structures? Does a preference for a particular orientation or value system represent a means test and is this tantamount to a creedal test?

4. Marginalization and Theological Identity

Theology is one of the most passionately held convictions of Unitarian Universalists. At the same time, theology is a sensitive and sometimes divisive issue with major implications for congregational polity. As a form of governance and an expression of our cultural ethos, congregational polity serves as a context for better understanding the multiple theologies in our movement. Although we do not have a creedal test or a dogma, we *do* have Purposes and Principles that help to make possible some degree of unity in our diversity. Unlike governance and issues on which a congregation can vote, different perceptions about theology can divide—and have divided—congregations in our movement.

While our covenant expresses our common mission as congregations, more specific issues not addressed in the Principles and Purposes surface as issues of congregational polity. For example, some members of congregations that have a dominant theological perspective fear that they will not be able to express freely their particular faith understanding and that their faith will be compromised. In an attempt to address both majority and minority theological views, some of our congregations have approached theology from "the least common denominator" perspective so as not to offend anyone. But this does not seem to be a solution.

As individuals, most Unitarian Universalists seem fairly reluctant, if not uncomfortable, disclosing or discussing their personal theology. While our collective acceptance of multiple theologies serves us well most of the time, our collective theological ambiguity sometimes acts as a point of division and conflict. If we are to reach a deeper understanding of the multiple theologies that we affirm as Unitarian Universalists, theological dialogue is needed, keeping in mind that while debate may promote mutual growth, it will not necessarily reduce fear.

A Non-Christian Religion?

Although both Unitarianism and Universalism are firmly rooted in the Jewish and Christian traditions, the Enlightenment has had a stronger influence on present-day Unitarian Universalism. Between 1930 and 1960, the primary theological identity of Unitarianism shifted from Christianity to various understandings of humanism and existentialism.[10] An apparent consequence of this theological shift was that Unitarian Universalism came to be widely known as a "non-Christian" religion.

It is true that *collectively* we are a non-Christian religion. A frequent interpretation of this non-Christian identity (both in terms of how we understand ourselves and public perceptions) has been that someone who is Unitarian Universalist cannot be Christian. While earth-centered theologies have been hotly debated on the General Assembly floor and in congregations, one of this century's most controversial theological issues in Unitarian Universalism has been whether one can be genuinely Unitarian Universalist and Christian at the same time. Indeed, one view is that it is a contradiction for a Unitarian Universalist to be a Christian. It is difficult to know how widely this view is held. We have heard vitriolic arguments on both sides, as in this statement:

> "Christian UU" or "UU Christian" is a contradiction in terms—or should be at any rate—and UUism ought not be cheapened by being linked to Christianity any more than it already seems to be.[11]

These perceptions and attitudes seem to prevail among many Unitarian Universalists and have been at the heart of several congregational and district-level disputes in which congregational polity became a central issue of contention. Some Unitarian Universalists who are not Christian presume that they know what a Christian is. And herein lies another problem: Neither what it means to be a Unitarian Universalist nor what it means to be Christian is easily defined. Further obscuring the debate are self-righteousness and some of our assumptions, habits, and communication styles operating within the marketplace of ideas, whether those ideas are informed or not.

Theological Biases

In spite of our fourth Principle—to affirm and promote "a free and responsible search for truth and meaning"—it seems fair to say that both anti-Christian and anti-Pagan biases exist among a significant number of Unitarian Universalists. With the adoption of humanism and existentialism as normative theological perspectives within Unitarian Universalism, the implicit message became: We support people in their theological search as long as they don't land at either end of the Unitarian Universalist theological spectrum with Christianity at one end and neo-Paganism at the other.

It is somewhat ironic that some humanists have begun to articulate their feeling of marginalization within Unitarian Universalism. Many who joined our movement before the 1960s, says the Reverend Suzanne Meyer, "often wonder whether they are losing their congregations, whether the style of religion they discovered in Unitarian Universalism still exists."[12]

It is difficult to say which theological perspectives are dominant in Unitarian Universalism at this point. What is clear, however, is that we are becoming a more theologically diverse religious movement. No doubt this trend stems from the fact that in the past 10 years, Unitarian Universalism has been in the middle of what a recent issue of the *World* magazine called a "tectonic shift,"[13] which presumably suggests greater diversity among Unitarian Universalists rather than a dominant theological trend. At least three factors have contributed to this shift in our theological understanding and identity:

- constant and predictable pendulum swings in religious ideas and movements the world over
- fewer new Unitarian Universalists who come with a deep commitment to anti-authoritarianism and religious freedom
- a longing for more spirituality among Unitarian Universalists.

While some humanists have expressed concern that more emphasis on the spiritual will lead to less emphasis on the intellectual,[14] the two are not always mutually exclusive. Our theological sensitivities, insensitivities, and misunderstandings continue to cause consternation that sometimes results in conflict about the issue of congregational polity. Four tendencies contribute to the conflict: prejudgment—our collective unwillingness to engage in serious theological dialogue or to understand what premises are held by Unitarian Universalist Christians, Pagans, and those of other theological orientations; a focus on points of difference rather than on points of unity as Unitarian Universalists; varying communication styles; and resistance to authority.

Other factors may serve as barriers to strengthening our common theological understandings:

- lack of clarity or a common definition of what theology is in its broadest sense
- lack of understanding or appreciation of the contextual and evolving nature of theology
- an unwillingness or inability to respect fully or learn more about theologies other than the one(s) we choose to claim

Barriers to strengthening our common theological understandings include an unwillingness or inability to respect fully or learn more about theologies other than the one(s) we choose to claim.

- an association of personal theology with creedal religion, doctrine, or dogma (particularly of the Judeo-Christian tradition)
- an inability or reluctance to reopen old wounds associated with past religious experiences.

These barriers—especially our resistance to authority and inability or unwillingness to engage in open and honest theological discussion without prejudgment—are also expressed in terms of social and congregational relations.

Comfort or Values: Which Do We Hold More Dear?

Conrad Wright, one of the most recognized authorities on Unitarian Universalist congregational polity, asserts that when we consider diversity, congregational polity is an "inherent" and "insoluble problem"; that congregationalism "inevitably limits the range of people who worship together." He states that "congregational polity is wedded to homogeneity"—that the more heterogeneous the group, the less likely it is that consensus will be reached on deeply held ideas. This stance is consistent with congregational studies from experts at the Alban Institute and challenges our assumption that diversity is both desirable and possible. Wright also assumes that racial and ethnic diversity is not sufficient common ground around which to unify the Unitarian Universalist movement and that the search for racial and ethnic diversity will be successful only if socio-economic unity already exists.

If these premises are true, our challenge is to find significant points of unity among us and ways to negotiate new structures on which to build our diversity. For congregations rooted in Presbyterian or Episcopalian polity, marginalized groups can appeal to a higher ecclesiastical body—and have done so with varying degrees of success—for participation and inclusion. In our congregational movement, however, there is no such higher body to promote empowerment for the marginalized. Tension within congregations has sometimes been increased by an emphasis on rights over responsibility and an affirmation of our values.

The challenges of liberalism are many, including the challenge to forge a greater degree of harmony between what Dr. William R. Jones identifies as our "espoused theories" versus our "theory-in-use." One such espoused theory, which is consistent with the first of our Principles (affirmation of "the inherent worth and dignity of every person"), is that our denomination welcomes all, regardless of race, class, nationality, and sexual or theological orientation. Yet because of the preponderance of people who fall within the UU norm—well-educated, middle-class people of European heritage

—it is not surprising that the assumptions, values, needs, and interests of the majority often prevail over the interests of the marginalized.

The Challenges of Democracy and Unitarian Universalism

At one level, the challenges of marginalized groups are directly related to congregational polity—the fact that our congregations are autonomous and can thereby choose to include or exclude the interests and needs of minority groups. At another level, the challenges of the marginalized are related to the premise that a representative form of governance (majority rule) is adequate for building democratic structures within our congregations. These issues are not unique to Unitarian Universalism, but they remain unresolved challenges of systems based on democratic principles the world over. We cannot dismiss the claims of marginalized groups simply by pointing to the fact that numerical majority groups almost always acquire and maintain more power than their minority counterparts. At one level, the quantitative measurement of participation in the Association is appropriate. At another level, however, a qualitative response is required if we are to achieve parity, if marginalized groups are to be heard.

More than 150 years ago, in his classic, *Democracy in America*,[15] French sociologist Alexis de Tocqueville articulated this dilemma. He argued that there is an inherent tension between equality and liberty in democracy that is not easily reconciled. He suggested that one of the challenges (and perhaps one of the limitations) of democracy is protecting the minority from the "tyranny of the majority." It is easy to focus our energies on those in our congregations whose strategies, tactics, or tone may be inconsistent with approaches that are comfortable for us. This phenomenon has been labeled the "tyranny of the minority." One tyranny is, of course, no better than another. But tyranny is not the issue. Rather, the processes out of which tyranny grows deserve examination. If, by the power of their numbers and norms, the majority in our congregations uses the democratic process of congregational polity to support and sustain injustice, oppression, and ultimately tyranny (in the hearts and minds of the minority), then the democratic process needs to be examined. If, on a consistent basis, the only way that minority groups can get the attention of the majority is to behave in ways that are dramatic, if not bizarre to some people, then some aspect of our system of governance is failing.

Using Theology to Guide Polity
Whether our polity guides our theology or vice versa is a question for seri-

ous discussion and consideration. Part of our challenge is to come to terms with our *religious* call and to let our religious principles guide how we approach the democratic process. If the Unitarian Universalist principles were our *primary* value consideration and the democratic process derived from those principles, Unitarian Universalism would look very different on the delegate floor at General Assembly. Exploring our moral, ethical, and religious premises in relation to political premises could shift the ways in which we view congregational polity, one of our most cherished principles.

If a dominant group has the power and numerical authority to name reality, to name the primary group identity, how can non-dominant groups ever assert their identity and their own empowerment? This is not merely a question of politics or of how we negotiate social relations. The politics of difference has both theological and political dimensions, whether or not the matter is placed within a religious context. Because religious institutions are endowed with greater moral authority than secular institutions, they are obliged and challenged to address these issues, though it may be "in fear and trembling," as Saint Paul suggests. Fear is not desirable; it is simply part of the human condition in moving toward change and in confronting our differences.

Balancing Power, Identity, and Difference

How marginalized groups negotiate power within the context of congregational polity is partly a factor of numbers. But increasing the number of groups now at the margins of our movement will not solve the issue of marginalization until we address a core assumption: that dominant group perspectives and experiences are normative in a hierarchy of values.

One of the favorite symbols among Unitarian Universalists is the circle. We invoke the circle to represent multiple elements of wholeness, relationality, inclusion, and diversity—suggesting that all are welcome in our circle. Once in the circle, however, there are still centers of power and margins of powerlessness. To emphasize the need for greater diversity is to overlook the interlocking relationship between those who have historically stood at the margins of our movement and those who remain at the center. Our failure to achieve greater diversity—present efforts notwithstanding—may be due in part to the fact that many of our congregations have focused on how to attract people who are "different" into the center, and how to assimilate them into the mainstream of Unitarian Universalism (which assumes an acceptance of the UU norm). By contrast, relatively little attention has been given to imagining what an authentic center would look like that included all who are now at the margins, if power within the circle were distributed more evenly.

> *Our failure to achieve greater diversity may be due in part to the fact that many of our congregations have focused on how to attract people who are "different" into the center, and how to assimilate them into the mainstream of Unitarian Universalism.*

If we are to transcend the paradox of identity differences in relation to congregational polity, we need to reflect critically on a series of questions such as:

- How do we understand ourselves in relation to "the other"?
- How can we move beyond what William Connolly calls "the dogmatization of identity"—carefully honoring the natural diversity of humans so that we are all empowered and we all value and respect our differences?
- How can congregational polity be structured and practiced in ways that are consistent with building the "interdependent web" and in ways that respond to the problematic relationship between identity and difference, inclusion and exclusion?

These are questions for congregational study and reflection on how systems of congregational polity function. Readers are encouraged to engage in what have been called "deep chair" discussions, a process that will invariably yield more questions, but more answers as well.

Summary

Both the theory and the practice of congregational polity sometimes impede our ability to move forward in serving the cause of justice, particularly as related to marginalized groups. If the cry of congregational polity is continually raised and successfully defended as a justification to exclude or diminish those groups that now stand on the edges of the circle of Unitarian Universalism, marginalized groups will never become part of the cultural center of our faith. How we negotiate different understandings and interests, and how marginalized groups can gain parity and empowerment—*in spite of congregational polity*—remains a core issue of our faith.

Recommendations

1. The UUA Board of Trustees should direct the staff to identify resources to strengthen congregational understanding of how our cultural ethos, collective identity, dominant attitudes, values, and norms within the Unitarian Universalist movement affect the empowerment (or lack thereof) of groups that are now marginalized within the Unitarian Universalist movement.

2. In our quest for "justice, equity, and compassion in human relations" and the affirmation of "the inherent worth and dignity of every person," the UUA Board of Trustees and staff should continue to support congregations in systemic anti-racism and anti-oppression training and educational initiatives.

3. In light of the fact that conflict is inherent in congregational polity, resources (such as referrals and training) should be made available to congregations for conflict management and resolution.

4. Congregations should reexamine their assumptions about democracy in relation to marginalized groups and the extent to which congregational polity is guided by Unitarian Universalist principles and values.

Sources

Conversations with Conrad Wright; Commission on Appraisal hearings; and Star Island Religious Education Week.

Notes

1. William E. Connolly, *Identity/Difference: Democratic Negotiations of Political Paradox* (Ithaca, NY: Cornell University Press, 1991).
2. Jung Young Lee, *Marginality: The Key to Multicultural Theology* (Minneapolis: Fortress Press, 1995), pp. 30-31.
3. Commission on Appraisal, *The Quality of Religious Life in Unitarian Universalist Congregations*, report to the UUA General Assembly, June 1989 (Boston: Unitarian Universalist Association, 1989), p. 31.
4. Barry A. Kosmin and Seymour P. Lachman, *One Nation Under God: Religion in Contemporary American Society* (New York: Harmony Books, 1993).
5. Jeanette Hopkins, "When Is a Welcoming Congregation Not a Welcoming Congregation," *Unitarian Universalist Voice*, Spring 1996, pp. 1, 6.
6. *Ibid.*
7. Commission on Appraisal, *EmPowerment: One Denomination's Quest for Racial Justice, 1967-1982*, report to the UUA General Assembly, June 1983 (Boston: Unitarian Universalist Association, 1984).
8. Jeanette Hopkins, p. 7.
9. *Ibid.*
10. Commission on Appraisal, *The Quality of Religious Life in Unitarian Universalist Congregations*, pp. 31-34.

11. John Sikos, "UUs Are Not Christians," Letter to the Editor, *UUDom: The Connection* (newsletter of the Unitarian Universalist District of Michigan), June 1996.
12. Warren Ross, "Diversity Without Division: Theological Difference in Our Congregations and How to Make It Work for You," *World*, November/December 1996, p. 36.
13. *Ibid.*, p. 34.
14. Carol Agate, "Uniting Spirit and Reason," sermon given at the 1996 Unitarian Universalist Association General Assembly in Indianapolis, Indiana.
15. Alexis de Tocqueville, *Democracy in America* (New York: Vintage, 1954).

SECTION TWELVE

Internationalism

The Unitarian Universalist Association has long been involved in internationalism. Collegiality with Unitarians and Universalists around the world; the call to education, service, and aid; and the increasing globalization of the neighborhood and world are among the factors that have motivated our efforts. The inevitable convergence of our polity—particularly when interpreted in a provincial way that questions whether we should extend any effort or assume any responsibility beyond our walls—with the very tangible, expanding, and complex reality of internationalism raises significant questions about who we are as a religious body and what our vision is for the future. This section describes international efforts of the American Unitarian Association, the Universalist Church of America, and the Unitarian Universalist Association; explores tensions that arise in the interface between congregational polity and internationalism; and suggests directions that the Association might take to enhance its work as an intentional religious movement, committed to excellence at home as well as abroad.

Why a section on internationalism belongs in a study of congregational polity is a legitimate question. For if we apply a narrow concept of congregational polity in which our form of government is limited primarily to the politics of autonomous local congregations, then the Unitarian Universalist Association's policy and practice with regard to internationalism is insignificant and only individual ventures in "encounter and response" are meaningful. However, if we grant the shortcomings of this constricted view of polity and understand the need to legitimize and develop the rela-

Throughout the nineteenth century the American Unitarian Association believed that it should propagate its form of Christianity among those not ordinarily able to hear it.

tions *among* autonomous congregations, especially in light of international missteps taken by the Association, then internationalism deserves our full attention and commitment. For, as the Principles and Purposes state: "We . . . covenant to affirm and promote . . . the goal of *world* community with peace, liberty, and justice for all. . . . The primary purpose of the Association is to serve the needs of its member congregations, organize new congregations, extend and strengthen Unitarian Universalist institutions and implement its principles."

The American Unitarian Association

The American Unitarian Association (AUA) maintained independent relationships with congregations abroad and international interfaith organizations. For example, beginning in the 1820s and continuing for a century, American and British Unitarians had missions to Calcutta, Madras, and the Khasi Hills of India. The Reverend Dr. Spencer Lavan described the mission as one of "encounter and response" and documented it extensively.[1] Key players included the "Father of Modern India," Rammohun Roy, and westerners, the Reverends William Adam, Charles Dall, and Jabez Sunderland. Lavan states, "Most Unitarians do not realize that throughout the nineteenth century the American Unitarian Association believed that, within the scope of its financial limits, it *should* propagate its form of Christianity among those not ordinarily able to hear it."

In 1900, the AUA under the leadership of president Dr. Samuel A. Eliot became a founding member of an interfaith organization that was named the International Council of Unitarian and Other Religious Thinkers and Workers (now known as the International Association of Religious Freedom or IARF). Its goal was nothing less than "the federation of nations, the brotherhood of mankind, and the peace of the world."[2] The International Council nurtured relations with other Unitarian organizations, such as those in Great Britain and Transylvania as well as with the Hindu reformed group, the Brahmo Samaj, in India.

In 1913 the AUA tried unsuccessfully to support the establishment of a mission church in Montego Bay, Jamaica, under the ministry of the Reverend Egbert Ethelred Brown, an African-American Unitarian.[3] In the era after World War I, President Eliot declared, "We are creating a new internationalism."[4] Indeed, in 1918 the AUA helped to call world attention to the dire plight of the Transylvanians under Romanian rule. In the early 1920s American and British Unitarians provided funds for the purchase of the Mission House in Budapest (now the second Unitarian Church) to be used as housing for ethnic Hungarians fleeing Romania. In 1921 the AUA supported the efforts of Charlotte Garrigue Masaryk, the wife of the president of Czechoslovakia, and the Reverend Norbert Capek and his wife to establish a Unitarian church in Prague. The AUA provided funds for the purchase of the building.

The Reverend Louis Cornish was president of the AUA from 1927 to 1937. In a history of Unitarianism, *A Stream of Light,* edited by Conrad Wright, David B. Parke provides a capsule of Cornish's presidency:

> Cornish excelled in international diplomacy. He traveled to distant congresses, there to mingle with representatives of other world religions. He loved the international protocol of robed processions, honorary degrees, and engrossed resolutions of greeting, never failing to inform the directors of an anniversary in Hungary or Japan.[5]

Cornish liked to travel abroad, but was not an effective administrator at home. He did, however, initiate an early version of the Partner Church project as well as publish on the dilemma of ethnic Hungarians living in Transylvania, which is still an issue today. (See Section 3, "Comparative Congregationalisms," for a discussion of the polity and history of the Unitarian Church of Transylvania.)

The presidency of Frederick May Eliot from 1937 to 1958 was characterized by a sobered sense of internationalism and great attentiveness to the Unitarian Service Committee (USC). During World War II, the USC worked primarily in Spain and France, helping refugees to escape from the Nazis and resettle safely. Following the war the USC sponsored work camps for youth in Europe, notably in Czechoslovakia and Germany. The American Unitarian Youth and the Universalist Youth Fellowship had extensive contacts with European counterparts such as the International Religious Fellowship.

The Universalist Church of America

The establishment of a Scottish Mission from 1876 to 1896 under the direction of the Reverend Caroline Soule marked the Universalist Church of America's first noteworthy engagement with internationalism. Previous questions about missionary work were apparently overshadowed by domestic issues. Henry Bowen, publisher of the *Universalist Magazine,* stated that he did not see much value in sending missionaries abroad when there was so much to be done in the United States. In 1821 he wrote, "Surely the soul of a *native* American ought to be as precious in our view, as the soul of a native of Hindoostan or the Sandwich Isles."[6] When B. Bowser, an African American Universalist, wanted to establish a mission in Cape Palmas in West Africa in the 1850s, Sylvanus Cobb, editor of the *Christian Free-*

man, was supportive. He encouraged the denomination to "send a band of well-qualified Universalist missionaries into heathen lands."[7] But no such support for Bowser was forthcoming.

According to historian Russell Miller, the Universalist Church of America continued to struggle with its commitment to mission in spite of a belief in "the oneness of the human family," but a supportive vote was taken at a General Convention meeting in 1882. Eventually, a "conversion of the converters"[8] began, evidenced at the World Parliament of Religions in 1893 in Chicago and again in 1907 with the establishment of a Commission on Foreign Relations and attendance at the International Congress of Unitarians and Other Religious Thinkers and Workers. The Commission reported that "instead of being simply a small and obscure church," the Universalists had become "part of a great world movement which has for its object religious freedom and human progress."[9]

After the opening of Japan, the General Convention of 1887 led by the Reverend Dr. James Chapin explored establishing a Japanese mission. Shortly thereafter funds were raised with enthusiasm from conventions and individuals. In 1890 the Reverends George Perin and Wallace Cate along with Margaret Schouler began their ministry in Japan. Perin wrote soon afterward: "I shall aim to multiply just as fast as possible through men [and women] who can speak the Japanese language. We must have Japanese preachers. I fancy the success or failure of our missionaries hinge here."[10] The Universalist Church of America in Japan was registered as *Dojin Shadan*, translated as the "corporation for all people," and experienced 35 years of moderate, though uneven, success. In 1928 Ryongki Jio, a Korean Universalist who had been educated in Japan, tried to start a Sunday school and social service center in Seoul. The center lacked financial support, however, and it is unclear what finally happened.[11] After World War II the Association of Universalist Women contributed greatly to the Universalist Church of America's rebuilding effort in Japan. Miller sums up the work of the mission:

> As small and even as insignificant as the Japan mission conducted by the Universalists since 1890 might have seemed, especially to those outside the denomination, it was indeed an "investment in Universal Brotherhood" of which Universalists could justifiably be proud. Always underfinanced, usually understaffed, and suffering from the slights and barbs of other denominations for most of its history, the Japan mission doggedly held on. The fruits of its efforts are difficult to measure, but at least to some Universalists they were worth all the effort and even sacrifice that had been expended.[12]

Despite occasional reluctance the UCA became involved with several significant missions as well as social service projects. Poor administration and lack of funding, however, seemed to obstruct their longterm success. Apparently the UCA never sought to *convert* its partners abroad in the narrow sense, but to *confer* a broad-minded, non-sectarian Christianity and to model the essence of its teachings.

Patterns of Internationalism at Merger

At the 1963 General Assembly, the president of the Unitarian Universalist Association, the Reverend Dr. Dana McLean Greeley, received support to open the first Office of Overseas and Interfaith Relations. The Reverend Max Gaebler was selected as its first director and was followed by the Reverend Max Kapp. Greeley and Gaebler traveled to Japan, the Philippines, India, and the Vatican, and to the International Association for Religious Freedom (IARF) Executive Council meeting in Europe. One result of their visit to the Khasi and Jaintia Hills, as it was called then, was the appointment of Devison Marbaniang as the first Church Visitor in 1965. It may be argued that his appointment has continued to play a positive role in the growth of the movement in the Khasi Hills to the present. Gaebler visited North American congregations to speak about the Association's international involvements. Greeley and Kapp also established an advisory committee.[13] During this period the UUA contributed up to two-thirds of the IARF's budget. In 1970 with encouragement from Greeley, the World Conference for Religion and Peace was established with the Reverend Dr. Homer Jack serving as its first director.

Of the Office of Overseas and Interfaith Relations, Greeley has written:

> From studies that were made we knew that the denomination as a whole regarded the Overseas and Interfaith Relations Department as a very low priority, or as not a priority at all, which seemed to me tragic, and symptomatic of a pathetic *provincialism*. If I hadn't wanted to keep the department for the wonderful work it was doing, I would have wanted to keep it to educate the denomination, or to counteract our provincialism.[14]

It is clear that internationalism played a *significant* role in Dr. Greeley's commitment to and vision of the inclusiveness of the Association. Some have said that he even took the Association "to an unprecedented high" in internationalism.[15]

In the late 1960s the office was closed for budgetary reasons and its work reverted to the UUA president. It appears that the Association's international response, beginning with the administration of President Robert

The Association's international response varied according to the policies and practices of the incumbent president and the respective boards of trustees and their level of funding.

West in 1969 and for the next decade, varied according to the policies and practices of the incumbent president and the respective boards of trustees and their level of funding. During this period the UUA president continued to be invited to serve on the board of trustees of the IARF, based first in Holland, then Germany, and now Great Britain. (The first full-time executive director of the IARF, the Reverend Dr. Diether Gehrmann, was hired largely with UUA funds.) Issues arose and were dealt with on a case-by-case basis. The Unitarian Universalist Service Committee (UUSC) and Meadville/Lombard Theological School carried heavy international responsibilities in their respective ways.

The Eighties

Interfaith and international involvement increased with the administration of President O. Eugene Pickett in 1979. From the beginning of his presidency Pickett displayed an openness and interest in the church growth movement. Perhaps part of the reason was that his administration had gained additional funds to allocate to internationalism through the Holdeen bequest. He served as an active member and president of the IARF through the late 1980s, encouraging formal UUA attendance at the meeting of the World Council of Churches in Vancouver, Canada.

The Reverend Dr. William Schulz, UUA president from 1985 to 1993, introduced a more aggressive stance toward internationalism. In 1988 he promoted a change in the Bylaws to admit overseas congregations, resulting in the admission of the UU Church of the Philippines. While the debate on the floor of the General Assembly polarized simplistically between those who professed to support global Unitarian Universalism and those who cautioned against potential "religious imperialism," the Bylaws were amended by the necessary two-thirds vote.

In 1988 Schulz and the director of the Department of Extension recommended to the UUA Board of Trustees the creation of Project India, largely funded by the Holdeen bequest. This program was to be based in Calcutta and directed by the Reverend Dr. Sunrit Mullick, a member of the Brahmo Samaj in India and a 1988 graduate of Meadville/Lombard. Project India was to coordinate the work of the Brahmo Samaj as well as the Indian Unitarians of the Khasi Hills, Madras, and Hyderabad. However, the project lacked congregational support without even an official UUA committee. By 1989 a quarter of the work of the Advocate for Racial Justice was devoted to international work. Internationalism was later shifted to the Department of Extension. Throughout there was no consistent recordkeeping or evaluation of Project India and the program was terminated by the next administration in June 1995.[16]

With the overthrow of the Communist Romanian regime in 1989, the Unitarian Universalist Transylvania Sister Church Project, founded for the spiritual and financial support of beleaguered Unitarians in western Romania, gained momentum and was coordinated by Moderator Natalie Gulbrandsen. Soon afterward the Association announced the gathering of overseas congregations in Prague, Warsaw, and Moscow. The Unitarian churches of Auckland, New Zealand, and Adelaide, Australia, which belonged to the British General Assembly of Unitarian and Free Christian Churches, also applied for membership in the Association. As a result the UUA Board of Trustees began to address issues of membership standards and international policy. President Schulz convened a World Summit of Unitarians in April 1993 in Budapest, Hungary, though without substantial input from those who had been calling for such a meeting. After five years without a written policy, the Board of Trustees in its last meeting with outgoing President Schulz in June 1993 approved a brochure entitled "International Policies of the UUA."

The Nineties

In 1993 with the election of President John Buehrens, a more decentralized stance on international policy and practice began to emerge. The position of special assistant to the president for interfaith and international relations, reminiscent of the post established by Greeley in the early sixties, was instituted and filled by the Reverend Dr. Kenneth Torquil MacLean. A *de facto* moratorium on international memberships was established by the UUA Board of Trustees. The International Council of Unitarians and Universalists (ICUU), chaired by the Reverend David Usher, was established in 1995 by the UUA to deal collegially and bilaterally with the issue of international membership and global Unitarianism and Universalism. The ICUU was created to share the responsibility with the UUA of deciding whether to admit Unitarians and Universalists in other countries to membership. The constitution of the ICUU declares its purposes to be "to serve . . . to affirm . . . to facilitate . . . to promote our ideals and principles around the world . . . and to provide [appropriate resources thereto]."

The IARF, which includes non-Unitarians and non-Universalists, was reorganized not only to support its executive director in the United Kingdom, but to enlist a United States coordinator, based in New York City. The IARF seeks to develop grassroots involvement in international efforts. When the administration gave indications of abandoning the Sister Church Program, the not-for-profit UU Partner Church Council (PCC) was formed in 1993 to serve not only the churches in Romania but also in Hungary and the Czech Republic. The Reverend Dr. C. Leon Hopper was elected as president and Dr. Judit Gellérd as first executive secretary. Of the PCC, which now holds an Independent Affiliate status with the UUA, the Reverend Dr. Hopper says: "I believe that the Partner Church Council is unique among UU organizations in that it is grounded on individual church connections and activities. It is church to church, truly grass roots."[17]

Present Efforts

Internationalism continues on the upswing, accompanied by a shift from the administration's centralization of authority and decision making to a more decentralized approach. According to Partner Church Council member, the Reverend David Keyes:

> As the mission field . . . moves closer to the local parish, the relationship of congregation and judicatory shifts. Congregations no longer look to headquarters for leadership and administration of international programs, or anything else. Rather, they look to headquarters for assistance and reinforcement in the agenda they have decided to set.[18]

Congregations no longer look to headquarters for leadership and administration of international programs. They look for assistance and reinforcement in the agenda they have decided to set.

In the last 30 years the UUA has continually been represented at meetings of the IARF. In addition, the Holdeen India Fund, under the directorship of Kathy Shreedhar, is dedicated to improving the conditions of the poorest in India. The Reverend Dr. Max Gaebler, who on behalf of the UUA visited India in 1995, writes:

> I was deeply impressed with Kathy Shreedhar's basic strategy in organizing and administering the program. She is always seeking, as she puts it, for people rather than projects. . . . [She] looks for individuals who already have something going, people of imagination and demonstrated ability whose commitment to "empowering the poorest of the poor" is abundantly evident. The grants she proposes are intended to provide organizational infrastructure and, in some cases, additional staff to enable these partners to pursue their chosen goals more effectively.[19]

The Unitarian Universalist Service Committee, which has noteworthy projects around the world, also acts independently and serves primarily non-Unitarian and non-Universalist constituencies.

In addition, about 20 people from various international religious groups associated with the IARF have studied at Meadville/Lombard Theological School, Starr King School for the Ministry, and Harvard Divinity School. Meadville/Lombard has had international students as far back as 1920.[20] The

Reverend Dr. Gene Reeves, former president and chief executive officer of Meadville/Lombard, comments about these international connections:

> Very often these actions by the schools . . . were a positive reaching out to establish long-term relations with people in other countries, especially Japan. . . . This was not done for the schools alone, but, in some sense I think, for the UUA. Of course, these were not actions by 25 Beacon, but I have never been willing to concede that "the UUA" means "headquarters." The UUA includes its members, including its closely related theological schools. The simple fact of the matter is that from an overseas perspective to send a student to Meadville/Lombard is to have a relationship with American UUs, and therefore with the UUA.[21]

The Church of the Larger Fellowship, which is affiliated with the UUA, has also tried to be accessible to its international members, pointing them to the nearest Unitarian or Universalist societies or to the International Council of Unitarian Universalists.

Congregational Polity and Internationalism

How has congregational polity affected internationalism in the UUA? In general, the president has made decisions, with the approval of the Board of Trustees, as to who will represent the UUA at international events and public meetings. In addition, when congregational input to international issues has been weak, administrative authority has been stronger and more autonomous. When there has been more international funding, as through the Holdeen Fund, there has been more activity and service work. With the current position of special assistant to the president for international and interfaith affairs, responsibilities may be brokered more easily between the UUA president and other groups such as the Partner Church Council and the International Council of Unitarian Universalists. The extent to which a wider network of Unitarian Universalists—such as those who are not part of the international network or cannot afford to attend international meetings and events—will be invited to participate is an important and as yet unanswered question.

Leadership in social service and advocacy has been lodged in the Unitarian Universalist Service Committee, the Holdeen India Program, the International Association for Religious Freedom, the International Association for Liberal Religious Women, the World Conference on Religion and Peace, and more recently in the Partner Church Council. In fact, the current executive secretary of the IARF, the Reverend Robert Traer, has made more social service initiatives a priority and has encouraged IARF branches around

Radical congregational polity seems to have worked contrary to broad-ranging and ongoing concern and support for international projects.

the globe to do the same. In 1995 the PCC issued a "Call for Action for Human Rights in Romania" concerning the denial of native language education to ethnic minorities. With an annual flow of $100,000 earmarked for Transylvania, this project may represent, to paraphrase the 1995 UUA presidential statement, "the greatest UU social activism since the Civil Rights movement." To the extent that individual Unitarian Universalists and congregations become involved in these associate member and independent affiliate organizations, they also become involved with international issues and projects of the Association.

The establishment of new churches and administrative programs has been the area of international work in which congregations have been least involved. Radical congregational polity seems to have worked contrary to, and continues to militate against, broad-ranging and ongoing concern and support for such international projects as the Reverend Egbert Ethelred Brown's church in Montego Bay, the Reverend Ryongki Jio's school and social service agency in Seoul, and the Reverend Dr. Sunrit Mullick's organization in Calcutta. After only a few years the projects of these clergy, who were duly fellowshipped by the AUA, the UCA, and the UUA, respectively, and who chose to minister in their homelands, were terminated for lack of financial support. Few individuals and congregations protested or perhaps even noticed the administrative terminations in these developing countries. The results might be considered racist and evidence of the continuing parochialism disparaged decades ago by Greeley.

Summary

The increased coordination of efforts by the UUA, between the administration and its constituents, among and within congregations themselves, would embody a broader, more democratic and humane congregational polity.

The current administration has initiated a number of constructive changes for the decentralization of power and greater grassroots involvement with internationalism, for example, the endorsements of the Partner Church Council and the International Council of Unitarians and Universalists.

The main congregational polity question is how issues about internationalism are to be decided. In the past it has primarily been by administrative initiative. Will the priorities be decided piecemeal by the General Assembly through resolutions presented by interest groups, or by the Board, or by the administration? How does our organizational form keep us from developing a coherent program?

The following questions need to be addressed:

1. To what extent do the congregations that compose the UUA want the Association to engage in international work? Do they prefer that this work be done by other organizations?

2. What are the UUA and congregations' relative priorities for international assistance (UUSC, Holdeen), extension (ICUU), and relationship (IARF, ICUU, PCC)?
3. Do the congregations support the administration and Board in moving away from admitting overseas congregations and toward building the capacities of the ICUU? Is it realistic to expect the ICUU to carry out international extension efforts?
4. Will existing overseas UU congregations be encouraged to create new associations or join existing ICUU members? Do we want to be internationally diverse?
5. At present, almost no UUA funds are spent internationally, except for support of the Special Assistant. Funding is from the UUSC, Holdeen and other bequests, and individual congregations through the PCC. Is the UUA to be primarily a representative to international bodies, like the ICUU and IARF?

In the future the increased coordination of efforts by the UUA, between the administration and its constituents, among and within congregations themselves, would embody a broader, more democratic and humane congregational polity. To quote Samuel Eliot, it would signal the long-awaited birth of a truly "*new* internationalism."

Recommendations

1. The UUA should retain and strengthen the position of the special assistant to the president for international and interfaith affairs.

2. The UUA should create an international committee, separate from the UUA Board of Trustees task force on internationalism, and including the special assistant as an *ex officio* member and experts in the international field. The committee should be empowered to act as an advisory group to the Association, to offer links with congregations, clergy, and laity, to educate congregations and institutions, and to keep the issues of internationalism at the forefront of our religious vision.

3. The UUA should encourage international committees at the district level, composed of members of congregations, the Partner Church Council, and the US and Canadian Chapters of the International Association of Religious Freedom. The committees should be charged with advising UUA trustees, district trustees, and executives; educating congregations on current international and interfaith issues of concern; and coordinating projects when needed.

4. The UUA, the ICUU, and congregations should provide longterm joint support to ensure more effective egalitarian missionizing models. Consistent record-keeping and written evaluations of the work should be maintained. An International Chalice Lighters program could be initiated in consultation with the ICUU to support international congregational and institutional efforts.

5. Issues of racial and ethnic diversity in the UUA should be examined in relation to our international work and should involve people with experience and knowledge of cultural contexts, language skills, intercultural and anti-racism training. "Ugly Americans" who have no serious interest or ability in engaging empathetically and deeply can obstruct internationalism in our Association.

6. The UUA Department of Ministry and denominationally affiliated seminaries should identify students who have the training and talent to do international work and who want to study abroad for limited periods of time. They should locate resources for them to do so.

7. Congregations and members should support the decision of the Board of Trustees to create the International Council of Unitarians and Universalists. Congregations and members should be involved with and keep informed of UUA representation to the ICUU. They should call for regular reports about the work of the ICUU through UUA trustees and the special assistant.

8. Congregations and individuals should support the Partner Church Council and encourage its expansion to other regions, especially East and South Asia, Latin America, the Middle East, and Africa. Congregations and individuals should increase financial support of the Partner Church Council to alleviate the need for PCC board members to pay their own expenses to attend business meetings other than UUA General Assemblies.

9. Congregations and individuals should support the work of the board of trustees of the US and Canadian chapters of the International Association of Religious Freedom as well as the establishment of new North American branches of the IARF in addition to those in Boston, Berkeley, Chicago, and New York. Congregations and members should attend the triennial IARF congresses and provide financial aid to encourage more multiracial and multiclass participation, not only from North America but from member groups around the world.

10. The UUA should promote significant growth in grassroots funding for the International Council of Unitarians and Universalists, the Partner Church Council, the International Association for Religious Freedom, and other international and interfaith organizations in addition to the Holdeen bequest.

Sources

Material in this section has been gathered from interviews and correspondence with: Richard Boeke, John Buehrens, Max Gaebler, Dr. Judit Gellérd, Donald Szantho Harrington, C. Leon Hopper, Jr., Homer A. Jack, David Keyes, Spencer Lavan, Kenneth Torquil MacLean, Sunrit Mullick, Abhi Prakash, Gene Reeves, George Williams, and David Usher.

Notes

1. Spencer Lavan, *Unitarians and India* (Boston: Beacon Press, 1977).
2. Russell E. Miller, *The Larger Hope*, Vol. II (Boston: Unitarian Universalist Association, 1985), p. 127.
3. Mark Morrison-Reed, *Black Pioneers in a White Denomination* (Boston: Skinner House, 1980), pp. 51-56.
4. Arthur Cushman McGiffert, Jr., *Samual Atkins Eliot, 1862-1950* (n.p., Claremont, CA, 1974), p. 13.
5. Conrad Wright, Ed., *A Stream of Light* (Boston: Unitarian Universalist Association, 1975), p. 120.
6. *Universalist Magazine*, 3, November 3, 1821, p. 75.
7. *Christian Freeman*, 23, July 5, 1861, p. 38.
8. Russell E. Miller, *The Larger Hope*, Vol. II, p. 417.
9. *Ibid.*
10. *Christian Leader*, 62, May 28, 1891, p. 2.
11. Russell E. Miller, *The Larger Hope*, Vol. II, pp. 452-53.
12. *Ibid.*, pp. 458-59.
13. Richard F. Boeke, letter, March 23, 1996.
14. Dana McLean Greeley, *25 Beacon Street and Other Recollections* (Boston: Skinner House, 1971), p. 58.
15. Gene Reeves, letter, April 5, 1996.
16. Sunrit Mullick, interviews, 1994 and 1995.
17. C. Leon Hopper, Jr., letter, July 1996.
18. David P. Keyes, letter, March 27, 1996.
19. Max D. Gaebler, letter to John Buehrens, June 13, 1995, p. 2.
20. Spencer Lavan, letter, March 25, 1996.
21. Gene Reeves, letter, April 5, 1996.

CONCLUSION AND GENERAL RECOMMENDATIONS

Toward a New Community of Autonomous Congregations

With this report the Commission invites Unitarian Universalists to embrace a new vision of congregational polity. We have called attention to the paradigm shift in liberal religious thought as a whole—from independence to interdependence, from individualism to relationalism. We believe that thinking of congregational polity only as a principle of local autonomy disempowers us. We believe that understanding congregational polity as the principle of "a community of autonomous congregations" empowers us and is more in keeping with our spiritual vision of who we are and what we seek to become.

We reaffirm the historic centrality of congregational polity within the Unitarian Universalist Association, its member societies, and its affiliates. But congregational polity brings out both the best and the worst in Unitarian Universalism. It brings out the best when it reminds us that power is ultimately in the hands of the membership, the people who are gathered in a local community. They know and depend on one another in many ways; they rejoice in one another and bear one another's burdens. They also exercise creativity and moral courage in ways that, as they know, few would do alone. They think of themselves as devoted Unitarian Universalists and the focus of their commitment and their giving has a name and address in their own local community. No wonder, then, that they take deep pride in the fact that they are self-governing and self-sustaining communities.

But congregational polity as we have understood and practiced it also brings out the worst in us. It does this when it invites us to look inward rather than outward, to go it alone rather than welcome the wisdom, aid, or examples of other congregations. Sometimes congregational polity seems

A new awareness of congregational polity as a community of autonomous congregations will strengthen both local congregations and the associations through which our congregations come together.

to justify a suspicious or hostile attitude toward external authority or higher ups. Even where attitudes toward denominational bodies or other congregations are highly positive, a parochial form of congregational polity often gives absolute priority to the local congregation's needs; financial support of denominational bodies, theological education, or ecumenical or community social-service agencies are not represented at the budget-negotiating table. The negative spirit sometimes infects the congregation; for instance, seeing its purpose in purely self-serving terms; treating the minister as a hired hand whose job is to please people; adopting an attitude that our group is for "our kind of people." An understanding of congregational polity that inoculates the congregation from accountability to other congregations, associations, and established ideals and standards allows such destructive patterns of thought and behavior to perpetuate themselves.

The Commission believes that a new awareness of congregational polity as a community of autonomous congregations will strengthen both local congregations as self-governing, self-responsible units and the associations through which our congregations come together and develop mutually beneficial relations. We believe that this practical goal can be secured through a broad range of specific actions, as detailed in this report. The matters considered in this report, though wide-ranging and numerous, are not exhaustive; other actions consistent with the same goal—to further the community of autonomous congregations—are important.

General Recommendations: Theory and Practice

We should propose amendments that reflect a more positive and less protective concept of congregational polity.

We make the following section-by-section recommendations for concerted study and discussion of congregational polity in theory and practice.

1. Theology
Congregational polity and practice should become the focus of our concerted theological reflection. The congregation should be seen as a mediating structure between the individual and the universal religious community. We should reflect and preach on the religious significance of being in community (rather than being in isolation).

2. History
We should renew study of the history of Unitarianism and Universalism relative to the origins of the congregational idea and evolving forms of governance. We should promote a fuller understanding of how congregational polity continues to evolve in response to new needs and spiritual awareness.

3. *Comparative Congregationalisms*
We should learn about the variety of forms that congregational polity takes among other religious bodies or denominations and the various polities found among Unitarian Universalists outside North America. We should enter into dialogue with others to overcome parochialism and to consider alternative models.

4. *The UUA Bylaws*
We should reconsider provisions of the UUA Bylaws that invoke congregational polity to ensure the independence of the local congregation and the provisions that establish moral or institutional commitments that are incumbent on all member congregations. We should propose amendments that reflect a more positive and less protective concept of congregational polity.

5. *The Ethos of Unitarian Universalism*
We should develop programs for congregations to promote in-depth discussion of the spiritual and cultural ethos of our congregations. We should examine the extent to which our ethos (our collective attitudes and patterns of behavior) is inward-looking and self-stereotyping, rather than outward-looking and open to the fuller diversity and vitalities of our communities, our world, and our present and potential membership.

General Recommendations: Pressure Points

We note the following section-by-section recommendations for harmonizing our understanding of congregational polity with our quest for innovative or reformed institutional programs.

6. *Congregational Life*
Each congregation should review its policies and procedures relating to internal governance, decision making, membership, and stewardship. The UUA should support and assist this process. Just as Fellowshipped ministers are held accountable to professional standards, so should congregations be held accountable to our Principles.

7. *Cooperative Relationships*
Forms of association and cooperative endeavor among congregations should be strengthened at all levels of the UUA—area, district, and continental. Congregations need to take fuller responsibility for the governance of intercongregational bodies and their official meetings (especially the General Assembly). The UUA should foster the decentralization of functions and joint ventures where possible.

Congregations need to take fuller responsibility for the governance of intercongregational bodies and their official meetings.

8. *Communications*

Communications among congregations, their members, and special interest groups in the Association should be steadily increased in quantity, accessibility, and frequency. Print media should focus more fully on serving local interests, concerns, and ideas. Media that focus on individual interests should reflect institutional interests as well. We must fully exploit the potential of electronic media. More of this work can and should be done at the local or regional level.

9. *Religious Leadership*

Ministry—professional and lay—needs to be understood as a function of the religious community, thus closely linked to forms of governance and accountability. Specifically, our separate categories of ministry should be unified. Community ministers should maintain a covenantal relationship with a congregation. The concept of ministry as a basic function of all members (shared or lay ministry) should be fostered. Students for professional ministry should be deliberately recruited and vocationally formed. The recent tendency to divorce the ordination of ministers from responsibilities to and from the ordaining congregation needs to be reformed, since it disempowers the congregation *vis-à-vis* the Ministerial Fellowship Committee. Community ministry needs to be affirmed by congregations as central to their larger ministry (service) to the world: by the same token community ministers need to be accountable to particular congregations.

10. *Social Justice*

Concerns of social justice and service should be fully owned by congregations (and not only individuals, committees, or special interest groups) as central to their corporate ministry to the world. Stands on issues of social justice that embody the moral and spiritual values in the UUA Principles should be enacted by the General Assembly and, on an emergency basis, by the UUA Board of Trustees.

11. *Marginalized Groups*

We must deal forthrightly with the fact that congregational polity often abets the exclusion of marginalized groups rather than welcomes them into the center of recognition and power. This is due in part to the predominance of white, professional, college-educated, middle-class people among Unitarian Universalists. To shift our perceptions of the Unitarian Universalist is imperative to our spiritual and ethical authenticity.

12. *Internationalism*

Vibrant interpersonal and institutional partnerships between our congregations and liberal religious bodies in other nations and continents (some, but not all, of whom carry the Unitarian Universalist name) are important links to the reality of a universal religious community. These relationships need to be fostered, especially at the level of the local congregation and its members, with keen awareness of the mutual benefits.

In all these ways the Commission is confident that Unitarian Universalism can become a new community of autonomous congregations. We believe that these recommendations are consistent with winds of change that are already blowing among us. We want this report to raise consciousness of basic institutional and spiritual concerns and to help us address various practical issues that need decision and action.

We urge Unitarian Universalists to take these matters to heart, to deliberate them with each other, and to act on them in ways that further our collective renewed vision of interdependent congregations.